How to T the 21st C ᴜᴛy

By Avoiding Porn and Other Distractions

TABLE OF CONTENTS

FOREWORD..4

INTRODUCTION.......................................7

PART 1: GATHERING INFORMATION

CHAPTER 1: WHY IS PORN HARMFUL?.........11

CHAPTER 2: FOUNDATIONS FOR LIVING A GOOD LIFE.......................................23

CHAPTER 3: WILLPOWER 29

CHAPTER 4: COGNITIVE BIASES...................45

CHAPTER 5: SUPERNORMAL STIMULUS.......65

CHAPTER 6: ADDICTION............................72

PART 2: BUILDING ON THE FOUNDATIONS

CHAPTER 7: WHO ARE YOU?...........................77

CHAPTER 8: PERSPECTIVE.........................98

CHAPTER 9: HOW TO TAKE CONSCIOUS CONTROL OF YOUR HABITS..............................103

CHAPTER 10: RELAPSES AND ENERGY SCALE..129

CHAPTER 11: ACHIEVEMENT AND NEUROCHEMIS-TRY.....................................142

CHAPTER 12: HOW TO GO FORWARD 150

FOREWORD

How does porn use affect your life? How do you become a successful person? How can you make your life better? The hidden synergies between becoming successful and ditching porn will be discussed in exquisite detail in this book. You will be given useful information on how your willpower, cognitive biases and other factors impact your ability to operate optimally. Many people lack a sense of purpose. I will show you how to get there! Success is in the eye of the beholder. Therefore, it is extremely important to find your values! Porn use is probably not your "real problem"; it is most likely only a symptom of a bigger, hidden issue, which is a lack of purpose. I will show you how I managed to end my struggles with porn and a lack of purpose, to ensure that you can do the same, no matter where you are in your journey.

Success is in the eye of the beholder. It is extremely important to find your values!

My reason for writing this book is not based on ethics, morality or religion. People can watch as much porn as they want. What people do in their personal lives is none of my business. I do however, believe that some people experience reduced quality of life from watching porn, and this is probably a bigger demographic than those who are consciously aware of the problems. Pragmatism has led me to write this book. It is challenging to notice the subtle negative effects porn use and excessive use of social media have on our lives over time. My goal is to open your eyes to how it can affect you, and if you resonate with the information presented, I hope that you will see the path going forward on how to regain control of your focus. If watching porn and masturbating for hours would help us accomplish our goals and live a happy life, I would happily endorse spending hours every day doing just that.

We should strive to be students of objective reality. The world doesn't care if we want certain things to be a certain way. Reality is going to persist longer than our delusions. People generally get what they deserve in life, not what they want. Watching porn and constantly experiencing artificial dopamine hits are not going to bring us any closer to deserve what we want. To get what we want, we have to work for it.

You can live a great life filled with meaningful experiences, travel, friends and family. You can also choose to watch strangers have sex online. Choose wisely. Read this book if you are serious about your outcomes in life. If you are unwilling to put in work, you should stop reading. Reading followed with inaction can result in cognitive dissonance, which only makes your situation worse. Feeling bad because you know what needs to be done, but not taking action is not a fun place to be in. If you are serious, continue reading. Implementing knowledge in your life is what produces results!

Most of the content of this book is based on scientific research. Personal experience and anecdotes are included as well, to present as much relevant information as possible. Internet porn is a new thing! We don't know all the ways it affects us yet. I have looked at porn use from many angles to understand its effects optimally. Reality is multidisciplinary and doesn't care about the confined space between academic disciplines. Life is complex. Therefore, I have researched disciplines such as biology, behavioral economics and psychology.

To understand a topic in real life, a multidisciplinary approach should be used. If you want to build a skyscraper, the building doesn't care whether the electrical engineers or mechanical engineers miscalculated something. If there is a problem, the entire structure will suffer. Medical science hasn't shown us that much about porn's effect on people yet. By showing the case from several angles however, I hope you will realize how big of an impact porn use and excessive stimuli in general, can have on our lives.

INTRODUCTION

My purpose for writing this book is to help people that experience difficulties with porn use and others that are unaware of the effect it has on their life, to live better. I have covered the principles and knowledge that I used on my journey. These concepts helped me go from rock bottom to living a happy and satisfying life. At age 21, I was in a bad spot with no aspirations or goals. I didn't have any hope for a better future. Eventually, I stumbled upon some videos on self-development on YouTube and caught a glimpse of a better life. Seeking out new information and pragmatically implementing it in real-life made my life turn around completely. In this book I have tried to reengineer the process I went through. I cover all the concepts, tricks and actions that helped me.

The last 5 years of my life have been devoted to researching how to overcome this addiction and how to live a better life. Through reading tons of books and trying out different things myself, I have tried to write everything here in a condensed and understandable format. I cover the mindsets and knowledge that helped me gain perspective and enough self-control to banish porn and distractions from my life.

The first part of this book will focus on what you need to know about porn and excessive stimuli in general. We do a deep dive into the science and psychology behind modifying behavior. What you should know about willpower, human psychology, addiction and more will also be covered to ensure that you reach your goals. This knowledge will benefit you greatly when you try to take conscious control later. Your time and secondly, your ability to use your time on the things you value are your most important assets.

In the second part of this book, we will explore how you should go forward to build the necessary focus to lock in on the things that matter to you. How do you become successful, and how you can live a life of your design? You will realize what you value the most, by completing a comprehensive exercise. Then, the tools to get there will be provided.

A lot of emphases will be placed on purpose and willpower in this book. These two key attributes are extremely important to change unwanted behavior. They also happen to be perhaps the two most important factors determining someone's long-term outcomes in life. Purpose is vital to know what to use your time on. Willpower determines if your focus will be used on these things or if you will be distracted. Today, there are so many distractions that it is easy to waste time on flashy things that only bring illusionary joy. To avoid this from happening, you need purpose and willpower. Sometimes, doing the right thing is difficult. By defining what you want to do with your life and staying committed to doing the maximum every day, you will realize that porn use will only reduce your ability to reach your goals. Willpower is the necessary ingredient that ensures that you follow through. If you feel like you have tried improving yourself many times, but never had the willpower to break through yet, don't give up! If you do the steps listed in this book, you will soon have the willpower to tackle any challenge you face in life.

The human brain has capacity limitations. To save time, we sometimes have to go away from fully informed decision-making and move on to automatic, primitive responding. When we are stressed out, we are more likely to rely on "mental shortcuts", like doing what other people are doing (social proof). We have created a highly stimulating and information-saturated environment. We are at an increased pace forced to follow these "shortcuts", because of the rapid change. Sometimes the consequences are disastrous. Our natural ability to process information is likely to become even more inadequate in a world of technological advances. Our mental apparatus is unable to handle the environment's complexity and diversity appropriately to make excellent decisions.

In a world of increased stimulation, some people and corporations can leverage our mental "shortcuts" for their benefit. Examples of this range from Facebook, Instagram to porn sites, which steal hours from people daily. Time is our most precious asset and these sites only provide temporary illusionary joy. People could be using their time in more rewarding ways, but since it is perhaps easier to use Facebook to fulfill social needs, they use it instead of socializing in person. Sometimes, corporations and websites profit from manipulating us. We should fight back hard every time someone tries to profit from our "mental shortcuts". We will probably only face more situations where people or companies are incentivized to steal our time in the future, and if we don't fight back, we will be left with less focus, time and energy to spend on the things that really matter.

You will get the most value from this book if you write down bullet points and engage in the exercises included. At the end of every chapter, I have written a summary of the most important concepts covered. I encourage you to make notes on these lessons. By doing this, you will take immediate action. Proactivity is extremely important if you want to change or do something in life. I have also included an exercise that will give you massive clarity going forward. It is called the 3 questions exercise. What kind of person am I? What kind of life do I want? Who would be good companions for that life? You will answer these questions in it. Failure to complete this exercise will result in a life filled with uncertainty and indecisiveness. If the concepts covered make sense to you, try to implement them. To achieve something, you have to take action first. Proactivity while reading this book is going to be a brick in your castle of success.

PART 1: GATHERING INFORMATION

CHAPTER 1: WHY IS PORN HARMFUL?

INTRODUCTION TO PORNOGRAPHY

The primary focus of this book will not be on the dangers of porn. Chances are that you are reading this because you already know that it is harmful. I will outline some important statistics, but the main focus will be on how you can quit and how you can transfer that success into other areas of your life. This book is written mostly for men, but women can benefit greatly from the lessons as well. The knowledge presented applies to everyone interested in living a better life.

Do you find yourself distracted? Do you catch yourself browsing mindlessly through Facebook and Instagram? Do you find yourself watching porn out of boredom? Do you wish you would be able to quit? Do you lack the willpower and determination to do so? Do you wish you didn't procrastinate and managed to be productive instead? Everyone struggles with some of these things to varying degrees. It is just that some are better or worse at it than others. We all delay working on that difficult project at times. Most of us waste hours every day on things like social media. We generally know what to do; it is just that we don't have enough willpower and urgency to do so. I think it is 3 ways to combat this. I will do a deeper dive on this later. The first way is to find out what you really value and write this down. Secondly, you must strengthen your willpower, and lastly, you have to realize your mortality.

You are going to die someday, what do you want to do

between now and then? Realizing your mortality will put your ego somewhat in check. Most of or all of our accomplishments come from some degree of cognitive dissonance. You don't step up because everything is perfect. You step up because you realize things could be better. Your ego is a structure that tries to convince you that everything is perfect already. Doing some soul-searching and resolving these kinds of issues will make you a more effective executor. It will help you transcend the ego's need for survival, and you will realize your deeper wish to thrive. Finally, it will make you capable of eradicating unwanted behavior such as procrastination and porn use from your life.

Internet pornography is not only extremely accessible these days, but constant exposure to sexual images is practically inevitable. Commercials, entertainment and news websites all contain pictures of half-naked at times and sometimes even fully naked people. Historically, graphic images only presented itself when an actual opportunity for mating was present. Today, these images are available everywhere. The instinct we possess to pursue all these sexual opportunities is how many end up addicted. The porn industry is massive, and many make tremendous amounts of money from it. Sexualized commercials increase revenue because they take advantage of our natural desires.

Just because sexual images are abundant, doesn't mean it is harmless. Our brains have developed in environments with scarce resource distribution, which is very different from what we are facing in the 21st century. There is a huge mismatch between what our brains have developed for and the massive stimuli we experience in our everyday lives. Evolution has ensured that the things we experience the most pleasure from also happen to be the most vital for survival, like eating and having sex. Finding a cheeseburger or visiting porn sites would be impossible for our tribal ancestors. Nowadays, the primal part of our brain wants to grip every opportunity it can, eating junk food every day and masturbating to porn for hours. Seeking instant reward is not what will produce the best outcomes in life.

Today, we get the best outcomes by delaying gratification. This is our willingness to delay reward by doing difficult things short-term to have optimal results long-term. Things like excelling at school or work, working out and eating healthy produce the best outcomes long-term. The problem is that delaying gratification requires building discipline and willpower. Building strong willpower, good work ethic and laser focus are among the most important things we can do to excel in the 21st century.

Porn can in some ways be more stimulating than sex with a real partner. Plastic surgery, HD, various angles, anime, lighting and digital makeup contribute to this. We are exposed to angles and zoom which simply wouldn't be possible during normal intercourse. With Internet access you have the option to see more naked hotties in the next hour than our ancestors ever did in their entire lives. Think about that for a second. If you watch hundreds of strangers copulate online every week, no wonder you have less motivation to achieve something.

A lot of our motivation for achievement is based on sexual drive. If you constantly waste your sexual energy on jacking off to porn, it will result in a diminished drive to go after sexual partners and accomplishments in real life. Your DNA thinks you are balling out of control and see no point in pursuing further goals. These dopamine spikes will reduce your motivation and make you less likely and willing to do the tough stuff that is required to get that premier life. Quitting porn can be life-changing. Your brain suddenly stops experiencing artificial dopamine hits and your situation is seen in an objective way. When the artificial dopamine spikes are gone, the brain will convince you to take action in real life instead. Before you know it, you are working hard towards new goals for the future. When you start to make progress, real joy, happiness, excitement and courage follows. Start your new life without porn today!

STATISTICS

Today, the highest estimates on how big the porn industry

is, say that it is a 97-billion-dollar industry (2018)! [1] Pornographic videos made up 27 percent of all online video traffic in 2018. [2]

Perhaps an even bigger issue is porn's ease of access. You can decide to watch it, and in mere seconds have it at your fingertips. This is one of the reasons why overcoming porn addiction can be so difficult.

Married couples that watch porn increase their risk of divorce by nearly 200 %. [3]

Porn addiction or problematic porn use affects 5-8 % of the adult population in the US. [4] Problematic porn use refers to an individual who self-identifies as addicted to porn because they feel like they are unable to regulate their porn consumption [5]. These people want to reduce their consumption because of various negative effects, but they are unable to do so. The population in the US is approximately 330 million (2020) and around 250 million are above age 18. If at least 5 % of the adult population struggles with problematic porn use, it affects 15 million or more, in the US only! This is only counting those who are willing to admit it is a problem. I think it is time for people to realize the severity of this issue and treat it accordingly! I hope I can bring more awareness to the problems many people face with porn in this book. For many, porn reduces their quality of life. The industry is massive, and many people experience personal - and interpersonal issues as a result.

WHEN DOES PORN GO FROM A BAD HABIT TO ADDICTION?

- Becoming secretive about usage.
- Irritability and anger as a result of a confrontation of use.
- Inability to stop despite negative consequences.

MANY SIDE-EFFECTS CAN OCCUR:

- Loss of motivation and drive.
- Sex without intimacy.
- Inability or lack of interest in attracting sexual partners.
- Decreased quality of relationships.
- Depression.
- Anxiety.
- Loneliness.
- Feelings of shame and guilt.
- Sexual dysfunction of various kinds.
- Divorce.
- Less time to focus on more important things.
- Objectifying people.
- Focus and memory problems.

Porn can have very many different side effects. Some people get away without any consequences. Some perhaps even feel that their quality of life is increased by watching it. Everyone is different and that is a great thing. For most people though, too much exposure to porn will result in negative consequences.

Porn use desensitizes us to our natural drives and makes us less likely to work towards a reward. When someone reaches age 16, he or she has probably seen hours of adult content online with people doing things they never thought were possible. This is something to think about. Porn is a massive experiment that we really don't know the consequences of yet. The research is limited, and the mainstream hasn't really acknowledged porn as a problem yet. I think that will change in this decade (writing this in 2020).

LOSS OF SEXUAL INTEREST AND REDUCED SEXUAL ABILITY

In 2010, a poll taken in Japan found that more than 36% of men aged 16 to 19 had no interest in sex. [6]

A study by Canadian researchers published in 2014 found that among 16 to 21-year-old males, 53.5 percent had sexual problems. 27 percent of the males that participated reported erectile dysfunction. 24 percent had problems with orgasm, and 10 percent reported low sexual desire. [7]

In Italy, a study looked at the impact of porn on sexual problems in men between 19 and 25. It looked at a ranking of sexual desire from 1 to 10 (10 being the highest). Porn users averaged a score of 4/10 while non-porn users came in at 8/10. [8]

One study reports that more men between ages 18 and 40 experience erectile dysfunction than men between ages 40 and 80! Think about that for a second. An analysis of previously conducted studies concluded that 2 % of men under age 40, experienced erectile dysfunction until 2002. This was before porn tube sites. The first one appeared in 2006. This enabled easy access to porn without downloading content. In 2001 and 2002, a big study examining thousands of European men between 40 and 80 concluded that about 13 % experience ED. In 2011, the same study was conducted on men between ages 18 and 40. ED rates among this group ranged from 14%-28%, an increase of 600-1300 % compared to a decade earlier! [9] This shows how common sexual problems have become and porn is most likely the biggest reason for this.

IMPAIRED DECISION-MAKING AND LOSS OF MOTIVATION

Increased porn use is correlated with a decreased connection between the reward center and the brain's prefrontal cortex (the area of the brain responsible for decision-making). This is associated with poorer decision-making and an inability to control impulses. [10]

Higher numbers of hours watching porn per week and more years of watching porn are correlated with reduced gray matter in the reward circuitry. This reduces motivation and impairs decision-making. Another side effect this is indicative of is reduced ability to feel pleasure. [10]

Researchers in Belgium looked at 14-year-old boys' academic performance twice and compared the two scores. They found that increased use of Internet porn decreased the boys' academic performance six months later. [11]

Even brief viewing of sexual images interferes with people's "working memory". This is the ability to mentally juggle and keep track of several items at once. [12]

EFFECTS ON RELATIONSHIPS

Researchers interviewed partners of "sexual addicts" (91 females, 3 males). This was done to learn how these people were impacted by the partners' use. The subjects reported feelings of hurt, betrayal, lowered self-esteem, mistrust, decreased intimacy, anger, feelings of being unattractive and objectified, feeling their partners had less interest in sexual contact, pressure from the partner to enact things from online fantasy, and feeling like they could not measure up to the content seen online. [13]

It is often recorded that children of a father that is addicted to porn, are indirectly affected because their fathers ignore them in favor of porn. [14]

In a survey of 400 Internet porn users, researchers added an online survey on eight pre-existing Internet porn websites to measure loneliness. The study found a big correlation between loneliness and Internet porn use, where the frequency of use was found to be the main predictor of loneliness. The second-highest predictor was time spent on additional use of the Internet. [15] Lonely people often try to fill the void by using porn or the Internet excessively. When the substitutes of porn or excessive use of the Internet are removed, people have to fill the void in other ways. This is where the massive change comes from. They typically become more social and outgoing and find healthy and fulfilling ways to fill the void.

Nearly two-thirds of attorneys at the 2003 meeting of the American Academy of Matrimonial Lawyers had seen a sudden rise in divorces related to the Internet. Of those, 58 percent were the result of a spouse using excessive amounts of Internet porn. [16]

CONCLUSION

I believe that most people can increase their quality of life by avoiding porn. Even though some people can get away without noticeable side effects, simply avoiding the unnecessary dopamine spikes can make their life experience more exciting and enjoyable. If these people manage to use the improved focus and motivation that comes with avoiding porn on productive things, I am certain that they can increase their quality of life. I know unhappy people that don't watch porn. Avoiding porn is not a magic pill that will fix everything. It is a great foundation however, for building a better life, and for some people avoiding it can make a world of difference.

Many people report becoming more at ease in social settings, after quitting porn use. Some people go years feeling tense and uncomfortable around other people. For some of these people, avoiding porn can mean a world of difference. I feel tremendously more comfortable around people after I managed to quit.

For optimal results, porn should be cut off altogether. Watching it once or twice a week is probably not going to leave your life in ruins, but it will have a negative effect. Remove porn completely from your life and try to never look back.

KEY LESSONS

- Porn is extremely abundant these days. Avoiding exposure to explicit content is very difficult.

- Porn use can affect relationships.

- Porn use can affect sexual ability.

- Porn use affects your ability to make decisions and your motivation.

- Avoiding porn removes unnecessary dopamine spikes, which makes your life experience doing other things more enjoyable.

CHAPTER 2: FOUNDATIONS FOR LIVING A GOOD LIFE

FULFILLING YOUR POTENTIAL

A person's outcomes in life are largely dependent on their ability to delay short-term gratification. A part of your day will be painful no matter what. The sooner you accept this the better. If you are willing to delay gratification and "eat broken glass day after day", you will get better outcomes than someone who always listens to their short-term emotions. People who always take the easy way out accept having lower income, lower net worth, and less cool experiences by doing so. You will have more chances to feel well your overall if you manage to care less about your emotions right now. Most things that bring real happiness require doing tough stuff short-term. Delaying gratification is necessary to reach the top of any field. One of the main benefits of avoiding porn is that it builds willpower and discipline. This will in turn make it easier for you to master other things in life as well. Having strong willpower will help you reach your academic goals, your financial goals and your health goals much easier. Developing this key attribute will set you up for success in all the areas you value.

If you accept some pain, your life will be much better. This is only in the beginning. The painful point is when you decide to do homework instead of watching YouTube. When the decision is made and you start to make progress towards your goals, you will experience the bliss that comes with doing what you know you are supposed to do.

Reading this, you have perhaps felt the negative consequences that porn use can have on your life. If so, I have good news for you. It is entirely possible to deal with the problem. Your current situation is a culmination of your actions in the past –

good or bad. You have the power to orchestrate the life you want going forward. No one cares more about your outcomes than you either. Your friends and your family don't care more about your outcomes than you. If you have been slacking off this can be a frightening thought, but it is true. Start caring about your outcomes, as no one else will walk the steps but yourself. You are the CEO of your life!

A common pitfall is assigning too much blame to yourself. Even though your current circumstances are a result of the decisions you have made in the past, until about age 20, you will be greatly influenced by your family, school etc. We are social creatures, and we are influenced massively by our environment. Your life circumstances growing up are mostly outside your control. So, realize that it is probably not your fault if you struggle with problematic porn use. We all have sex drives, and porn is so readily available these days that it is almost impossible to reach adulthood without having been exposed to it. Exposure turns into a habit for many. Simply picking up this book is a great step in the right direction. We can't change the past. The best way to deal with the past is to simply accept it. Realize that the only thing in our control is what happens from now on. Therefore, let go of the past and try to remove feelings of shame and guilt if you have that. Look towards the future instead. Your future is what I will help you take control of in this book!

MAINSTREAM MEDIA AND HOW IT REINFORCES BAD HABITS

Internet porn is widely portrayed as both normal and socially acceptable in our day and age. For this reason, it can be very difficult to connect viewing porn to sexual difficulties or other issues. Perhaps your physicians or articles online told you your struggles were related to something else. Many authoritative voices out there will tell you porn use is healthy and completely normal. I think this is because of how new online porn is – we don't know all the consequences yet and how severe they are.

When I first started to feel some negative effects porn use can result in, like social anxiety, decreased motivation and worsened focus, I did some research. What I found was articles in mainstream media claiming porn use is healthy. Various professionals wrote these articles, so I trusted their guidance at my detriment. From then on, I succumbed further into porn addiction. My life got progressively worse. At this point, I knew something wasn't right and I started looking for more information online. I eventually realized that my problems could be caused by obsessively watching porn when I found the resources nofap.org and yourbrainrebalanced.com. Without knowing, I would have been unable to address the problem. Therefore, I am tremendously grateful for the effort the people behind these websites have put in.

SUCCESS

As previously mentioned, being exposed to porn in the first place is not your fault. It is completely natural since we are sexual creatures and the content is easy to access. It is difficult for a teenager to suspect that it can be harmful. It is however our responsibility as men or women to handle this. None except you is going to fix your problems for you. You can find help, but you need to realize that this is your mission, your responsibility and that no one can walk the steps for you. I encourage you to seek help, guidance and accountability because this is proven to be the easiest way to handle problems. If you were smart enough to figure it out by yourself, you would have done so already. If you want to learn to play the guitar, finding a teacher will cut your learning curve. It is the same way with this. Michael Jordan had 10 coaches at the peak of his career. Look for mentors that can help you reach your goals. If avoiding porn or doing nofap is among them, congratulations on investing in yourself. Seek out other resources and mentors that can help you reach your goals faster as well.

To succeed at anything, you must have the right secret

sauce. If you want to achieve something great, you must re-peatedly act, learn from your mistakes and continue through adversity. If you lack resilience, you will not make it through difficult periods. Success is a recurring theme in this book. The reason for this is that avoiding porn and/or doing nofap are things we do to excel and improve. People do it for various reasons, but the common denominator is aspirations to become a better per-former in one or more areas of life; basically, to become more successful. For me, the biggest reason was overcoming social anx-iety. For others, it can be attracting sexual partners, becoming happier, developing better social skills or simply stop wasting time. I am going to cover the synergies between all these things. Avoiding porn or doing nofap is a lifestyle, and if you want to do it successfully for a longer period, you have to become a stronger version of yourself. This will translate into other areas of your life as well. I am here to guide you along the way. Good luck!

KEY LESSONS

-       Take responsibility for your current life circumstances. At this point, your life is the culmination of your thoughts and actions in the past – good or bad.

-       Realize that most of your decisions - good or bad, have been impacted greatly by society and your environment. We can't change the past, but we can steer our direction going forward. Accept the past and be determined to take control going forward instead!

-       Since there is little research on porn use, mainstream media portrays it as something normal and unproblematic. Even your physician might tell you porn use is healthy.

-       Avoiding porn is something that people become interested in because they want to succeed or have better results at something. How can this success be translated into other areas?

CHAPTER 3: WILLPOWER

WHY DO YOU NEED TO LEARN ABOUT WILLPOWER?

The reason why willpower is so important is that it allows us to say yes to the things we really want, and no to the things that don't matter. This implicitly means that for willpower to have any true meaning, we must know what we value. What is so important that I can sacrifice almost anything for it? What is not important to me? What should I not use my time on? What should I use my energy on? When these questions are answered, and the required willpower to follow through is present, immense progress towards your goals will follow. This is how success happens. Let's dive into willpower.

We skim through Facebook instead of delving into our big project. We watch Netflix instead of doing our homework or reading a book. Achievement requires willpower. It is exhausting to achieve and constantly withstand our impulses. Strengthening your willpower will make you get more things done and make you stand out from the crowd positively very quickly. Most people are constantly distracted and addicted to their cell phones. If you manage to build your willpower and use that extra time on something productive, you will look awesome by comparison in no time.

WHAT IS WILLPOWER?

Willpower is defined as one's ability to control desires, attention and emotion. When you have defined what you want, your strength of willpower is perhaps the biggest factor determining if you reach your goals. Your outcomes regarding health, relationships and personal finance are hugely dependent upon this ability. Willpower is one of the most important (and least talked about) factors determining your life-quality. To succeed at self-control, it is important to know how it works and how we normally succumb to temptations. Therefore, we will cover the science behind it and how you can get more of it.

Many people think that willpower is simply resisting temptation. Willpower also involves saying yes though; Saying yes to the most important things at the expense of other things. You must have the awareness of knowing what really matters to you, to differentiate the importance of different activities. The tricky thing is choosing priorities since most of us want to do a lot. To reach your top goals, you have to neglect the rest. Even things important to you will have to be neglected if you are going to be excellent at something. Failure to understand this will result in mediocrity at best.

Self-control is often referred to as stopping yourself from doing something your primal brain wants. Willpower is commonly referred to as putting all your attention into succeeding at something. Willpower and self-control go hand in hand. If we build the part of our brain that is responsible for long term decisions, we will develop both our self-control and willpower. Self-control is a better predictor of academic success than intelligence. [17] If we train our brains to delay gratification, our outcomes will be better. Simple as that.

Self-control is a better predictor of academic success than intelligence.

Avoiding porn (or doing nofap) will help you build strong willpower and great self-control. Training yourself to withstand temptation, will turn you into a badass. It is going to aid you in all areas of your life. Whether you are studying for a test in school, working on a major project or want to clean your house, having strong willpower will help you finish the task quicker with less mental effort expended. You only get to work on your willpower when it is not convenient. This means that the time when you really don't want to go to the gym is when it is most important to go. This is the time when you will strengthen your willpower the most. Following through at these times will build champion neural pathways. Your willpower is something you can only work on when you don't feel like it. Keep this in mind the next time you want to postpone or cancel something because you are tired. Build a track record to yourself of following through at times when you don't feel like doing something. You have the opportunity to build champion neural pathways or weak-ass neural pathways, choose champion ones!

Our neurochemistry works fascinatingly. Every time we substitute something with leisure, we become more liable to make excuses the next time as well. When you go do the thing anyway, you make it easier to go do the thing the next time as well. Your brain basically keeps a tally of how often you do what you are supposed to do, and reinforcement makes you more likely to be a champion today if you behaved like a champion yesterday. This is because of neuroplasticity. Our brains can form and strengthen new neural connections throughout life. This means that your actions affect your neurochemistry. If you start to act like a champion, your neurochemistry will adapt and strengthen pathways that reinforce champion outcomes. The old saying "fake it till you make it" is true scientifically to a certain extent at least.

Your willpower is something you can only work on, when you don't feel like it.

Science has shown that each use of willpower makes the self-control system less active in the short-term. A study showed an interesting correlation between blood sugar levels and willpower. Participants who consumed a glucose beverage behaved less aggressively than participants who consumed a placebo beverage. Depleted blood sugar results in less willpower than having high blood sugar levels [18]. The reason for this is that self-control is one of the most energy-expensive tasks the brain can perform. Self-control consumes a lot of glucose. It is one of the first things that we cut (or reduce) when facing low energy supplies. This is done to make sure that we control our emotions and focus our attention which are more critical tasks for survival.

There is a reason we love chocolate so much. Most human (and mammalian evolution) had scarce resource distribution, meaning that it was important to take advantage of the few opportunities that came. People who live in an environment of excess are guided by taste to over-consume caloric dense foods. Following this tendency without exerting some willpower often results in diabetes and obesity. [19] Low blood sugar makes us access the primal part of our brain. This also makes us much more likely to relapse to porn for example. Therefore, it is beneficial to eat foods low on the glycemic index (convert carbs into glucose slowly) and avoid foods that give huge spikes and drops in blood sugar. Having stable blood sugar levels helps you maintain self-control.

Self-control is one of the first things that we cut (or reduce) when facing low energy supplies. This is to make sure that we control our emotions and focus our attention, which are more critical tasks for survival.

It is beneficial to eat foods low on the glycemic index (convert carbs into glucose slowly) and avoid foods that give huge spikes and drops in blood sugar.

We basically have two brains. One is impulsive-driven and wants fun and pleasure right now. The other is constantly planning and wants to make good long-term decisions. If you delay gratification and say no to temptation all day, you can suddenly find yourself watching several tabs of porn in the evening, thinking what the hell happened? What happened is that the part of your brain that is responsible for willpower got taxed. Willpower is an instinct we have developed evolutionarily to protect ourselves from the dangers that come from being too lazy. So, we have two different instincts that have opposing interests, and the one that is the strongest wins.

Willpower is like a muscle. If you constantly train it, it will become stronger. In the short-term, after doing something taxing, it will be temporarily weakened. You will run out of motivation before you run out of willpower. Willpower is something that can't be completely depleted. It just gets much harder to run that extra mile when you have finished a marathon already. Willpower is increased with increased motivation. If you remind yourself of why you are doing something, your willpower will increase, particularly if there are strong incentives. Imagine if someone paid you 1 million dollars if you avoided porn for 3 months. You would probably do anything in your power to avoid it. I would surely be willing to live in a tent in the wilderness for a few months if I was compensated 1 million dollars for it. I would argue that quitting porn use is worth more to you than 1 million dollars. If you can harness strong inner motivation, you will increase your willpower tenfold.

If you remind yourself of why you are doing something, your willpower will increase, particularly if there are strong incentives.

Wise people value their time above anything else. Time is our most valuable asset, so don't waste it. Wasting your youthful moments watching porn is not optimal. If you don't value your time, you don't value your life! If you were 90 and you were given the choice to go back to your youth, you would not only scrape together every penny you could find, but you would probably use all you could borrow as well! Your time is so precious that you should be really stingy with it.

It is very important to set goals the right way. Goals should be big and shiny. If it is easy to reach your goals, you don't need to work hard for them. As a result, you will probably waste a lot of time on leisure. If you had bigger goals, you wouldn't have the luxury of doing that. This means that your life will be suboptimal, compared to what it could have been. You are basically accruing debt in the background of the opportunity cost of the things you could have been doing if your goals are too small. Setting goals the right way will result in increased willpower.

Working constantly probably sounds like a chore to most people. If you are working on something you don't value, it is. Spending your time on tasks that propel you towards your goals is completely different. It simply doesn't feel like work anymore. You gain a real sense of accomplishment and real satisfaction if you are working on something that brings you closer to your goals. It is a much better feeling to spend your afternoon after work on a project you are passionate about than wasting it watching strangers copulate or watching TV mindlessly for hours. If you currently waste a lot of time on leisure, don't flip out. I have spent years of my life doing just that. I didn't have any good mentors that could help me out. Find your values and stick to that. We will go into this in chapter 7.

Ask yourself before doing something: "Is this something that I want to be doing every day? Do I want to procrastinate by not starting on that book project, every day for the next year?" Do I want to feel the consequences of not doing nofap every day for the next year? Every time you feel like indulging or doing something that goes against your long-term goals, asking yourself a question along these lines will serve you well. This trick is from Howard Rachlin who is a behavioral economist. [20] Thinking about what would happen if you do or fail to engage in a given habit, every day for a year make the consequences much more pronounced. You will see the result of your behavior much more clearly. Our psychology is not wired to see cause-and effect-relationships easily.

If you drink a bottle of soda once, it doesn't have a significant impact on your health. If you drink one bottle of soda every day for a year, it will be bad for your health. Every time you feel like giving in to temptation, asking yourself what would happen if you did it every single day for a year can set you up for great success. We are not trained to go around seeing the big picture all day. Most of us only think a couple of weeks ahead. By doing this trick, you will circumvent some of your inherent ignorance. We have many weaknesses in our psychology which I will do a deeper dive on later.

When the brain recognizes an opportunity for reward, it releases dopamine. What happens next is that we feel awake and alert. We are willing to work to reach the promised reward. If your dopamine system is ruined, you are not going to work to reach a reward. This means that your willingness to work towards favorable outcomes will diminish if you engage in habits that ruin your dopamine system. You will still feel pleasure if you reach the outcomes, but they will simply not happen because a lack of dopamine means that you don't have the necessary willingness and desire required to reach them.

Everyone knows that they are more likely to ace a test if they study for weeks compared to the last night only. More hours put in, with no difference in quality, equals better results. Simple as that. If you have a healthy, well-functioning dopamine system, you will be willing to put in more hours to reach your goals.

In general, social media and cell phones are very addictive because they take advantage of our reward systems. Video game designers intentionally manipulate our reward system to keep players addicted. Many of the cleverest people of our time are using their talent to figure out how to make people addicted to technology (video games, cell phone apps, movies, Google, Facebook, Instagram, etc.) The overuse of cell phones is to a large extent driven by the desire to connect socially. People use social media instead of seeking out social encounters because other people also spend their time there. It is easier to send a friend a message online than to show up in real life. This already results in pronounced consequences. For many, it results in less social contact.

Social media and Instagram in particular, can be risky to use for people struggling with porn use because of something called the habit loop. The habit loop explains how browsing

Instagram can result in gradually seeking out more explicit content. Before we know it, we suddenly find ourselves viewing hardcore content. Exposure to half-naked models is difficult to avoid if you browse through Instagram. The dopamine spikes from this exposure can make the brain turn to old neural pathways of addiction. Not having a social media presence at all will likely leave a lot of opportunity on the table these days. This is because everyone is using it, and it has become an integral part of how we interact with each other. Be aware of the downsides, and don't let yourself be run by it though. Try to consciously avoid situations where old, destructive habits can be engaged (such as browsing through Instagram mindlessly).

After experiencing a dopamine spike, we are more likely to look for instant gratification. For example, if you go to the supermarket and an attractive person is handing out free chocolate, there are different stimuli at hand (free, attractive and chocolate.) This makes it much more likely that you will buy unhealthy options afterward. The brain has been promised reward and will look for something to satisfy it. It even makes it more likely that we will book a vacation or go to the spa, as the brain has been promised reward (dopamine spikes). The brain is willing to go far to materialize reward.

Seeing models on Instagram is not going to help you quit porn. The brain is promised reward by dopamine spikes, and it is liable to seek out more explicit content to fulfill the promise. Obviously, we don't want to live without any stimuli either, but being aware of this is very important. Being aware makes it easier to avoid falling prey to attempts at swaying judgment. Be aware of what you allow in your life and remove unnecessary stimuli. Your brain will try to reach reward in counterproductive manners frequently if you fail to do this.

Marketers take advantage of our psychological tendencies. There is a reason why pictures of half-naked girls are abundant on news sites and workers hand out free pizza at supermarkets. Marketers know that this provides us dopamine spikes, which in turn makes us seek reward they can make money from. Even looking at bikini photos will give you a dopamine hit. Your brain will try to satisfy the promise of reward. Going to the nightclub and seeing real men or women is different, as your brain will still experience a dopamine hit, but the way to reach reward in the real world is to attract a partner. If you sit behind a computer, the easiest way to satisfy the promise is to jerk off. Your brain is wired so that it "needs to fulfill the promises" it is given. Make these promises come from real people, not strangers online.

Dopamine makes us chase reward regardless of obtained satisfaction. I can personally think of numerous incidents when I relapsed to porn. I would experience way less pleasure than anticipated. The pursuit of happiness is dopamine's main goal. Giving in to the temptation of relapse is going to bring you way less pleasure than you think. It will also reduce your chance of reaching your long-term goals. So, don't do it! If you try to revisit the pleasure from giving in to a craving and compare it to what you may be "promised by your brain", the magical spell wears off. It is almost certainly a huge gap between the promised pleasure and the experienced one in the past. Your brain is assigning disproportionate amounts of pleasure to the things you crave compared to objective reality. Relapsing is not worth it.

Depression and apathy are in many ways similar to how the brain works when the reward system is not functioning properly. Apathy results in reduced incentivization to act. There is simply no desire, willingness or hope present for a better future when a person is in an apathetic state. People who binge on drugs or pornography can experience this in the aftermath. In this state, there is no motivation or fire in the belly to go do something. If you look at the opposite side of the spectrum, on highly motivated people, they tend to have a healthy reward system. By reducing exposure to unnecessary stimuli, you will draw more happiness from the things you value, whether it is your partner, friends or hobbies. If you stay up all night and watch porn for hours before meeting your friends for a coffee break the next day, it will probably give you less pleasure than usual.

By reducing exposure to unnecessary stimuli, you will draw more happiness from the things you value, whether it is your partner, friends or hobbies.

Visual stimuli are increasingly abundant and more difficult to avoid. You must separate real rewards that give your life meaning, from false rewards that keep you distracted and addicted. Being able to see this distinction and acting accordingly will greatly influence your quality of life. Imagine what the future will bring. It is probably going to be even worse in this aspect. If we fail to take conscious control of our attention now, we will most likely be even more addicted to technology tomorrow. Start now!

You must separate real rewards that give your life meaning, from false rewards that keep you distracted and addicted. Being able to see this distinction and acting accordingly will greatly influence your quality of life.

The most common way of dealing with stress is to engage in behavior that activates the reward system. This is because dopamine promises us that we will feel good. Real-world stress increases the chance of relapsing. This is true whether we are talking about a drug addict or a pornography-addict. Normally, a person becomes "convinced" that what he or she is addicted to is the only way to feel better in times of distress. Some women concerned about their financial situation shop to alleviate their concern. [21] Yes, you read that right. To cope with feelings of distress, they add more debt to their credit cards. Learning about cognitive biases makes you less prone to making irrational decisions like this. People do completely irrational things facing stressful situations. Among the most effective stress-relieving strategies are exercising, socializing, reading, meditating, walking and being creative.

When we are stressed, our brains mispredict what will make us happy. You have probably experienced this yourself. Imagine that you arrive home after a stressful day at work. Your brain can tell you it is a good idea to watch TV or engage in other mindless things. After having watched TV for hours, you probably feel just as bad or only slightly better. If, on the other hand, you do something that requires an initial effort like going for a walk or going to the gym, you will feel much better afterward. A great way to remind yourself is to write down how much better you feel after doing the healthy habit instead of the pleasure-seeking one. Our impulses are not to be trusted when you are stressed. Try to remember this the next time you feel some distress. Go for a walk in the park or meditate. You will thank yourself later.

When we fail to live up to our expectations and do the thing, we feel guilty. Slipping on a goal can trigger your brain to crave dopamine. The best way to counteract this is to forgive yourself for slipping. Let's realize it; no one is perfect. People that don't forgive themselves after slipping, generally go into a downward spiral that only makes the situation worse. Self-compassion should be practiced when you feel weak. When you feel strong, keep going. Sometimes it is good to be a little harsh, but other times it is beneficial to realize that we are not perfect. If you relapse, there is no point in digging yourself further down. Get your head back up and soldier on. The past is not in your control. The future on the other hand is in your hands!

People that don't forgive themselves after slipping, generally go into a downward spiral that only makes the situation worse. Self-compassion should be practiced when you feel weak.

KEY LESSONS

-       Willpower is your ability to say yes to the things that really matter at the expense of other things.

-       Your willpower is something you can only work on when it is not convenient for you. It is like a muscle, and it can be temporarily taxed.

-       Willpower is reduced when facing low blood-sugar levels. Eat foods that provide stable, lasting energy to maintain good self-control.

-       Reminding yourself of why you are doing something will boost your willpower.

-       When considering giving in to temptation, ask yourself if this is something you want to do every day for the next year. The consequences of the action will become much more pronounced for you. Doing this can help you stay strong.

-       A healthy reward system (healthy dopamine levels) will make you capable of working harder towards your goals.

-       Be careful with your exposure to stimuli. A stimulus that releases dopamine makes the brain chase reward. If you look at bikini photos on your cell phone, the easiest way for your brain to fulfill the promise of reward is to seek out more explicit content online.

-       Start working on your willpower and self-control now. The future will most likely bring even more stimulating devices and content, so it will only become harder to regain control if you wait.

-       When you are stressed out, the brain wants to engage in behavior that activates the reward system. Dopamine promises that we will feel good. Some of the most effective stress-relieving strategies are exercise, socializing, reading, meditating, walking and being creative.

- If you relapse, be kind to yourself. The best way to avoid binging is to forgive yourself.

CHAPTER 4: COGNITIVE BIASES

COGNITIVE BIASES

A cognitive bias is a systematic deviation from rationality. An example is our tendency to overvalue our performance. Most people think they are above-average drivers. Humans are by no means rational creatures and many factors impair our judgment. Cognitive biases can be viewed as "shortcuts" our brains rely on. We make about 95 % of our decisions based on "mental rules of thumb". These automatic thought patterns have been developed because they allow us to make quick decisions that have proved to be valuable. It is in your best interest to make a snap decision if a tiger is running towards you. Being aware of the most important cognitive biases will be a great tool to possess in your pursuit of happiness. When several of these biases occur at the same time and cloud our judgment, disaster can follow. Many examples can be found almost daily of people falling prey to various kinds of human misjudgment.

Constantly reading about these biases and reminding yourself of them in perpetuity, will not only help you live a better life by seeing reality more objectively, but it can also help you abstain from porn. It is almost as if you develop the ability to watch yourself from a distance and you stop doing stupid things like watching porn. I am going to outline the different biases, their implications and how they relate to porn or your life in general. If you change a thought in your head, you will change your behavior.

The human brain is extremely advanced and complex, but science has shown that the brain is only capable of processing a certain amount of information at any given time. [22] This means that for the brain to process information effectively, it has to make certain "assumptions". The people that are most vulnerable to manipulation are the ones who think they can't be manipulated. Famous experiments and events that can be explained by cognitive biases include the Milgram experiment, German soldiers under WW2 and many more. Most people believe they would rebel and refuse to partake in the genocide of WW2. Would you rebel? Well, those who truly rebelled were less than 1 in 10 000. This is not meant to depress you, but to enlighten you on the power of the combinatorial effects of cognitive biases. Only by learning about them, you can transcend them.

SELF-LICENSING

License to sin is the use of a good deed to cover up a bad act. [23] Self-licensing is a cognitive bias that enables people to justify immoral behavior without it affecting their self-image of being a moral person. People who are asked to donate to charity give less if they recall donating previously. [24] This human tendency explains how you permit yourself to have something unhealthy for dinner because you went for a workout earlier. At times, it can be wise to "sin" by doing something of little importance to you. Let's say your primary goal right now is to quit porn, and you generally try to eat healthily, but it is not a big concern at the moment. If your willpower is temporarily weakened (by lack of sleep etc.) it can be a good idea to order Domino's. If you feel like there is a chance you will relapse, giving in to a "lesser sin" enables you to use moral licensing to your advantage. Paradoxically, it is important to be aware that it is only inconvenient situations that enable you to strengthen your willpower. So, as a word of caution, only use this trick when it is absolutely needed.

A sustainable solution to avoid the pitfall of licensing to sin is to untie your goals from being good. Let's face it, we have all eaten a huge cheat meal after going to the gym. This can be avoided by seeing the intrinsic value that comes from working towards your health goals; endorphins or becoming healthier. Staying on the path can be rewarding by itself; you don't have to reward yourself because you manage to do so.

TEMPORAL DISCOUNTING

Temporal discounting is our tendency to devalue rewards in the future. The strength or lack of this tendency explains our ability to delay gratification. The human brain has a very strong bias towards right now compared to longer-term outcomes. Different parts of our brain light up when thinking about our future selves and our present selves. The same parts of our brain are activated when thinking about other people and our future selves. This means that we treat our future selves as different people. Think about that for a second! When given a choice between 50 dollars today and 100 dollars a year from now, many will choose immediate 50 dollars. [25] Good luck finding a guaranteed 100 % return annually.

The human brain has a very strong bias towards right now compared to longer-term outcomes.

People grossly misjudge their time. Most people can't even predict a future self, more than 6 months ahead or so. A normal person doesn't really have a concept of self, in terms of how their behavior today is going to affect their outcomes long term. Perpetual focus on short term emotions ruins lives.

Temporal discounting applies to porn use. Discontinuing porn use after a long time involves enduring a few tough weeks initially and then a couple of months with some uncomfortable moments. After this, it is basically effortless. You just have to maintain the habits and momentum you built during the first month or two. Since humans in this regard are irrational creatures, many of us would prefer to live a lesser life than our potential, to avoid a few weeks of hardship. That is sad.

Temporal discounting applies to things like working out or starting reading books as well. Most habits that will make your life better in the long run, are difficult to stick to initially. It is basically a barrier to entry. We make lousy deals with ourselves only to feel pleasure right now. If people can't possibly predict accurately how decisions right now impact the future, no wonder so many of us end up watching too much porn.

Delaying rewards 10 000 BC was probably not the best idea. Our brain is programmed to indulge when an opportunity shows up because opportunities were so scarce historically. That is why avoiding porn when sexual content is so readily available is difficult. In prehistoric times when the opportunity for reproduction presented itself, you would be foolish not to seize it; it could be very long till next time. If you managed to find some honey, you should probably eat as much as possible and then some more.

A study has shown that children can be trained to improve cognitive control. This improved cognitive control tracked academic results as well. [26] By building your self-control, you can improve your ability to delay reward, which means your long-term outcomes will be better! The most successful people in the world can delay rewards more aggressively than normal people.

Temporal discounting rates have shown that drug addicts have a much higher discount rate than most. This means that they can't effectively delay rewards in the future. A study looked at this and compared an opioid-dependent group with a control group. Among the controls, a hypothetical reward of 1000 dollars lost 50 % of its absolute value after 37 months. The opioid-dependent group on the other hand felt the monetary amount lost half its value in 4.5 months! [27] Right now is really a crack-head idea!

If the world favored people that only want pleasure right now, I wouldn't be writing this. I would be watching some HD porn. The world favors people who educate themselves, learn skills and accept that the best things in life come from hard work. Simple as that. Your ability to delay gratification will to a large extent determine whether you will become homeless, highly successful or somewhere in between. The homeless guy sleeping on the beach, probably just wanted some pleasure in the short-term. See where he ended up!

*Your ability to delay gratification will to a large
extent determine whether you will become homeless,
highly successful or somewhere in between.*

We have a predisposition to think that everything will be easier tomorrow. This is our default way of thinking. We will have more time and money. Everything will take care of itself and all the problems I have today will magically disappear. It sounds stupid when I write it out like this, but it is our default way of thinking about the future. We procrastinate and delay things, expecting it will be easier tomorrow. Waiting will only make it harder.

We are creatures of habit. If you prolong the time before you take action, it will reduce your chances of reaching your goals. Your brain's neural pathways become more ingrained by the action or inaction you take. It will be more difficult to change when the neural pathways become more ingrained as time goes by. If you want to change something, now is the time. I used to be a victim of this mentality regarding my social anxiety. I remember thinking that everything would magically turn around someday. I thought I would eventually find myself in easier life-circumstances. I thought I would get the required motivation and willpower to work on it, out of the blue. That day never came. It only got worse until I finally realized that the day I was looking for, was never going to come. I realized I had to take responsibility and start taking action if I wanted a different outcome. If you want to accomplish something, you have to work for it. There is no other way. If you want to become a millionaire or get six-pack abs, perpetual procrastination is only going to make it harder and less likely you will get there.

We think of our future selves as different people. We won't take on responsibility today but have no problem burdening our future selves with massive work and responsibility. Our future selves are imagined as superhuman. Your future self has a bigger appetite for difficult tasks than your present self. Although it might not seem pleasurable in the short term, caring about your future self is the easiest way to become successful. People that are aware of the future and planning for it, instead of pretending that they will be 22 forever, will probably have a better future because they are more willing to delay instant gratification since they are aware.

Feeling disconnected from the future version of ourselves gives us permission to discard and neglect the consequences of our actions today. On the contrary, trying to identify with your future self makes you less likely to indulge in your worst impulses. Don't be a dick to your future self. Start taking your future into account and picture yourself 5 or 10 years from now. What would your future self be grateful you did now?

Some people tend to plan at the expense of the present moment constantly. These people don't value the current moment, which is our only access to life. This is called hyperopia. So, what you want to do instead is work hard and celebrate when you deserve it. In practical terms, this can mean working your ass off during the week, putting in long hours at work, hitting the gym and taking care of an important project in the evening. But when the weekend comes, take the time to relax and spend time with your friends and loved ones. The reason we want to delay gratification is to optimize the present moment in the future.

If we continually try to optimize but never enjoy the moment, we miss out. If we only worry about the present moment and discard the future's value, we also miss out. This is because our future selves will be in a worse position than it could have been. So, try to find your sweet spot. For me, this means working my ass off most of the time and then taking the time to relax and have fun, when I have something to celebrate. It is a reason the word celebration is commonly used for parties etc. If you haven't done anything, you don't have a reason to celebrate. A common side effect of answering the 3 questions (an exercise in chapter

7) is that you will begin to find working towards your goals enjoyable. When you know exactly what you want to accomplish within different areas of your life, it won't even feel like work. It will become enjoyable.

People that manage to delay gratification have better lives in almost all aspects. They are more popular, have better academic success and manage to handle stress better. The more a person discounts a delayed reward, the more likely that person is to have a range of behavioral problems, including clinical disorders. [28] Out of nothing but sheer selfishness, it is important to consider the wants and needs of other people and help them reach their goals. By doing this, more will come your way also. We generally get what we deserve.

LOSS AVERSION

Loss aversion refers to people's tendency to prefer avoiding losses to equivalent gains. According to Daniel Kahneman people feel on average 2,2x more pain from losing something compared to acquiring something. This impacts tremendous amounts of decisions in all areas of life. From a rational standpoint, this doesn't make any sense. You can use loss aversion to your advantage though. Reach your long-term goals by applying an interesting trick. Imagine the future and the reward you can enjoy if you behave in the right way. Then think to yourself if indulging right now is okay, knowing that indulging ruins your future payoff. For example; Imagine your future payoff by avoiding porn being a healthy and fulfilling relationship with a partner (and you don't have that now). Is it worth it to watch porn right now, if that is going to reduce your chance of having that perfect relationship later? The reason this trick is so effective is that it takes advantage of loss aversion bias. We don't want to lose something, so we can go great lengths to avoid it (whether it is something imagined or real).

Imagine your future payoff by avoiding porn being a healthy and fulfilling relationship with a partner (and you don't have that now). Is it worth it to watch porn right now, if that is going to reduce your chance of having that perfect relationship later?

OPTIMISM BIAS

Perhaps the most important cognitive bias that we possess is optimism. Optimism is mostly beneficial, and it is important for self-preservation. There are however situations where it is much better to look at things objectively. Think of trying to avoid porn. We have a strong predisposition to positivity. This can sometimes border on delusion. A common way of thinking is that things will magically work themselves out. We think it will be easier to deal with our problems tomorrow, and we mispredict how our current behavior will affect our future.

A problem will most likely persist or get worse if no changes are made. Think in terms of health and fitness. If a person is obese and continues to engage in unhealthy habits regarding nutrition and exercise, the person will probably be in an even worse spot in the future. This is the case for just about anything. You may tell yourself that you will never relapse again. If you don't make any changes, you will relapse again. Fact. If you want to modify your outcomes, you have to make some changes.

If you work on the wrong things, you will only get worse. You would have figured it out already if you were smart enough. Be humble. Einstein's definition of insanity is engaging in the same behavior expecting different outcomes. Most of us are doing this in one or more areas of our lives while being unaware. If you plan for success with avoiding porn, you have to change some habits. You can't simply do what you have always done and expect to be strong enough to handle urges suddenly. This is how optimism can be detrimental.

Sometimes, people cannot assess their situation objectively, and they think they will get rich or extremely fit in the future with doing not much. That is not how success happens. If you want to avoid porn (and you have been unable to do so previously), you have to make some changes. You have to start doing things that you have not been willing to do in the past. Stuff like stopping watching television, picking up meditation and generally accepting some pain in the short-term is required. More on this later.

SOCIAL PROOF

Social proof is a way of measuring value based on people's perception. It allows us to make quick judgments based on other people's opinions. This is a great thing in many ways. It allows us to save time. My favorite movies almost always have a rating of 7,5 or higher on IMDB. This means that other people have found it enjoyable too, and I don't have to do extensive research when considering what movies to watch.

Social pressure is the pressure we feel in social situations to fit in. If you can't tolerate some social pressure, I have bad news for you. If you constantly let how other people think affect you, your life will be nothing compared to your potential. This even applies to quitting porn. Most people are not aware of the harmful effects of porn. If you tell 100 people that you try to avoid it, I would guess that most people find you weird for doing so. Sometimes you have to go against what most people think. How can you go for what you really want as a unique person, if you allow everyone's opinion to affect you?

Standing out from the crowd is something we fear. Doing this in a tribal setting 10 000 years ago could potentially put us at risk of being abandoned. Today, most of the dangers of standing out from the crowd are gone, but the fear persists. Everyone should try to work on their ability to tolerate social pressure. If you feel that your culture or society is doing something wrong, you will go with the crowd unless you are strong enough to stand up for yourself. There are tremendous amounts of examples in history where terrible crimes were considered normal in various cultures. It is not enough to simply be aware. To live by your values and morals, you must have the ability to tolerate social pressure. When this ability is present and you know what you value, you can go for what you want!

Being unable to tolerate social pressure makes you the equivalent of a human jellyfish. You just float around with the current where there is no friction. Tolerating social pressure is required if you want to become successful in many areas. To become a good investor, have good communication skills and much more, you need this ability. When the market is down like it was in 2008, big money can be made. The problem is that you have to distance yourself from crowd psychology to capitalize on market crashes. "Be greedy when others are fearful and fearful when others are greedy" – Warren Buffet.

> *"Be greedy when others are fearful and fearful*
> *when others are greedy"* – Warren Buffet.

I used to have issues with alcohol when I was younger, and I frequently got way too drunk. Going from the guy that was the most intoxicated to not drinking at all, meant I had to deal with intense social pressure. I would have been trapped and unable to rectify my behavior if I had not cultivated the ability to tolerate social pressure.

Social proof is such a strong force that it even impacts our reasoning abilities regarding life and death. Cialdini describes something called the Werther-effect in his famous book Influence. When the media covers suicide, more suicides and even accidents than usual follow in the aftermath. The same thing happens with mass murders. The concept of social proof mostly affects people in similar situations. What happens after a head-line about for instance suicide, is that people similarly situated sees suicide as a "legitimate path", since it is reinforced by other people doing it. Now, something this extreme is not going to happen to most people. But social proof affects all of us. Many people's lives are ruined because of this effect. Be yourself! Laugh in the face of people trying to apply pressure of conformity to you and your actions.

CONFIRMATION BIAS

A person that wants to live a better life, should strive to constantly learn new things. It is very important to expose one-self to ideas and beliefs that go against one's current understand-ing of the world. We tend to discard information that doesn't support our current beliefs. We generally only accept informa-tion that reinforces our current beliefs. Therefore, it is unwise to voice strong opinions based on little information. When we voice opinions in public or in front of other people, there are many strong mechanisms at play that make us try to live up to people's expectations. One should always try to understand real-ity as objectively as possible.

Reality will persist longer than your delusions. If you hold on to inaccurate and suboptimal beliefs for too long, you will only build debt in the background, consisting of the opportunity cost of the things you could have been doing. This means that you will lose out on life and opportunity for every month or year you hold on to inaccurate beliefs. Therefore, it is of the utmost im-portance to read and try to learn new things. Expose yourself to ideas and information that contradict your current beliefs. This will make you view life and matters in a more objective light, which means you will spend less time doing stupid things.

PSYCHOLOGICAL DENIAL

Sometimes, the reality is too painful to bear, so we distort it until it is bearable. This is a pervasive psychological tendency, and all of us have it to various degrees. Many addicts deny that they have a problem. Many people that experience issues with problematic porn use or addiction deny it as well.

CONSISTENCY AND COMMITMENT TENDENCY

This is your enemy trying to make a better life for yourself. Your DNA doesn't necessarily want you to win. First and foremost it wants you to survive. Due to loss aversion among other things (fear of losing your current situation), it is difficult to step up. This bias has severe consequences when trying to step up and make a better life for yourself. Even unfortunate circumstances are difficult to change. A part of you will try to stay there, because of familiarity. Your DNA knows that your current behavior is enough to survive. Therefore, it doesn't want to risk adopting new behavioral patterns. Your brain is afraid that an alpha man will beat your head in with a rock if you become more social, louder and more expressive. This fear is rooted in evolution, but today it is irrational.

People that have been thinking a certain way for a long time, will have massive difficulty in accepting new evidence that discards their previously held beliefs. A common example of this is people that have never worked out and experience health issues in their senior years. It is oftentimes more painful to accept that time has been wasted engaging in suboptimal behaviors than to accept objective reality. In extreme cases, some people would rather die than accept previous shortcomings and waste of time. Don't allow yourself to become a victim of this. Another example of this is commonly found in science. If someone presents a new theory that challenges commonly accepted beliefs, they face massive resistance. It is normally a new generation of scientists that accept the new evidence since it is so difficult for the older ones to discard previously held beliefs.

THERANOS

Theranos was a company that tried to make small automated devices that could diagnose people for a wide range of diseases and medical issues by blood testing. If they had been successful, they would have revolutionized the medical industry completely. The company managed to raise more than 700 million American dollars from investors. The founder Elizabeth Holmes intentionally misled people. She had them believe that Theranos was on the verge of a breakthrough and lied about revenue figures, among other things.

Behind all this lies a cautionary tale of the combinatorial effects of cognitive biases. Holmes was deeply passionate and extremely determined to make her vision come true. She fell prey to a "lollapalooza" event", where several cognitive biases intersect and cloud our judgment. It basically makes the human brain turn into mush. What she did is to a large extent only human nature. The more we can be aware of these tendencies, the more of our inherent irrationality we can remove, setting ourselves up for lasting success.

Incentive-caused bias makes people with a vested interest in a project believe more strongly in it. This can cause a condition known as "motivation blindness". It affected both the investors and the founder of Theranos. Furthermore, the people involved were affected by the tendency to be blinded if something seems preeminently important and the tendency to be blinded when trying to create something new. People are a lot more liable to do unethical conduct when it is for a good cause. This also affected Theranos and played a role in its downfall.

By learning about these biases, we can stop ourselves from making suboptimal decisions in our own lives. These biases are "mental shortcuts" that have developed with evolution, and they can hinder rational decision-making. Making rational decisions is a prerequisite for living an optimal life. This is pretty clear. If you let your emotions guide your actions instead of logic and your future goals, good luck avoiding porn, as your emotions will tell you it is a good idea to watch it several times a day!

IN THE AFTERMATH

If you manage to stop watching porn, many psychological biases will play against your favor in the aftermath. With added motivation, clarity, purpose and desire to achieve something, you will have to tolerate social pressure when you try to expand. Many people report becoming more social in the aftermath. You will have to face resistance from commitment and consistency tendency, by going against what people expect from you in social situations to make the change last. We resist change and it can be difficult to make it permanent. If you want to quit watching porn, you have to change. If you are addicted to porn, your current level of consciousness "needs" the stimuli. To reach a state where porn is not "needed" anymore, change must happen. You have to reach a point where you obtain so much enjoyment from day-to-day life (without extreme stimuli like porn) that porn and other highly stimulating things are simply not needed anymore.

People report on average, that the most important factor in their lives is their relationships with other people. We are social creatures, so this should come as no big surprise. To live a happy life, I think everyone needs good relationships. I couldn't communicate and relate effectively to other people when I was younger. This is perhaps also the reason I fell prey to porn addiction myself. I had to learn to become a more social person and how to relate better to other people. Learning this enabled me to receive more happiness from my relationships, which in turn reduced my need for compulsive behavior.

People report on average, that the most important factor in their lives is their relationships with other people.

When being around my old friends and family trying to quit porn, I experienced discomfort when trying to build a new identity. It is uncomfortable to go against what people expect from you. When you try to quit porn, cigarettes or other harmful activities, cognitive tendencies will try to pull you back to a level of homeostasis. Many of the tendencies and biases can be circumvented by building your tolerance to social pressure. Many cognitive biases take advantage of social dynamics, so if you manage to tolerate social pressure well, the natural pull from them will be reduced.

COGNITIVE BIASES AND PORN USE

Do you want short-term pleasure at the expense of long-term outcomes? Start taking your future into account. Do you want to suffer for 1 month trying to quit, or suffer for the rest of your life? Start taking your future into account.

Consistency makes us more liable to follow through on something that we tell others. Consider seeking out accountability to quit porn. We want things to stay relatively the same, regardless of whether the current situation is good or bad. This tendency makes you resist change regardless of your current circumstances.

KEY LESSONS

-       We have certain systematic deviations from rationality that have been programmed into us by evolution.

-       Doing a good act normally results in people allowing themselves to misbehave afterward.

-       The human brain has a very strong bias towards right now compared to longer-term outcomes.

- Start relating to and picture yourself in the future. Doing this will make you take your future self into account and make you more capable of delaying gratification.

- Most people have no concept of their future self, more than 6 months into the future. Don't be a dick to your future self.

- Take advantage of the fear of loss, by picturing that you have achieved something you really want. Now, your fear of losing something (imagined or real) will make you capable of working harder to avoid it being taken away from you.

- If you don't change any of your current behaviors, your life will stagnate and get worse.

- Train yourself to withstand social pressure. Failure to do so will make you turn into a human jellyfish, only going with the current and unable to follow your deepest dreams and goals.

- Be willing to let go of your most beloved ideas. Humans have a strong bias towards confirming what we already know and discarding ideas that go against our current way of viewing the world.

- Humans have a strong tendency to live up to other people's expectations. Train yourself to tolerate social pressure to reduce this effect.

CHAPTER 5: SUPERNORMAL STIMULUS

"Supernormal stimulus" is a phenomenon where artificial stimuli can change evolution. Examples include candy, porn, junk food, the Internet and video games. Internet use recruits our natural reward system but potentially activates it at a higher level than the levels of activation our ancestors encountered. [29] This is a recipe for addiction.

Stimuli from the screen change our preferences to match what we watch, and this creates new pathways for arousal that are unnatural. This weakens the natural genetic response. Some people would rather watch porn than have sex with a real partner. Every time we watch porn, we strengthen pathways for arousal that counteract the natural one. So, for every video we watch, we ruin our enjoyment and willingness to meet real people.

Every time we watch porn, we strengthen pathways for arousal that counteract the natural one. So, for every video we watch we ruin our enjoyment and willingness to meet real people.

There are some dangers to Internet use. One element is present with all Internet use. We can maintain or heighten arousal by googling or finding new stimuli in perpetuity. A click on the mouse enables us to experience renewed arousal. Scanning for salient cues in the environment furthers survival. It activates the brain's reward system. So, this means that continually looking for the "perfect porn scene" or googling random stuff in perpetuity, activate the reward system.

The Coolidge effect is a phenomenon that explains how porn use can become problematic. Men are programmed by evolution to seek out many sexual partners since this is likely to increase the chances of reproduction. Whenever a new potential female sexual partner is introduced, sexual interest is renewed. This is something that porn sites take massive advantage of. Some people spend hours masturbating, looking for the perfect video to climax to.

All drugs of abuse affect our reward system. Eating and having sex activate the reward system since these activities are necessary for our survival. The universal effect of drugs is a flood of dopamine to our reward center. What follows is a positive response to the behavior that caused the spike in dopamine. Our brain then rewires to adjust, making it more likely that we will engage in the same behavior in the future. In other words, anything that spikes our dopamine - be it drugs, sugar or porn, makes our brains want more.

Porn users often binge. Many also watch YouTube videos for hours or surf the web for hours after porn use. This is normally done to avoid the negative effects of withdrawal and to experience continued stimuli. After a session like this, just sitting on the couch without stimuli can be painful. This is a state a lot of people find themselves in these days. If we remain unconscious and allow ourselves to experience overstimulation for a long time, our everyday lives become dull and sometimes outright painful.

Today, meeting a romantic partner involves socializing. Going to the bar, having a few drinks and socializing with new people is a common way of trying to find suitable options. You will probably not find your dream partner the first night out, so persistence is key. This means that you have to delay gratification to find your desired partner. Porn on the other hand, gives you pleasure instantly without putting in work. You can find your favorite content with a few finger swipes in mere seconds. This means that watching porn will make you less capable of finding your ideal partner, as you build suboptimal neural pathways that reinforce instant gratification. If you want to succeed at finding a great mate for you that matches your preferences, you will probably have to talk to more than one person. When you are opting out by watching porn, you reduce your chances of honing social skills and other attributes required to find a good partner.

This means that you have to delay gratification to find your desired partner. Porn on the other hand, gives you pleasure instantly without putting in work.

"Supernormal stimuli" reduce your dopamine response to normal activities. Simple things like going for a walk or doing your morning commute, will be much less enjoyable if you over-stimulate your neurochemistry. After a porn binge, I remember feeling no pleasure from the small things in life. Sometimes they felt outright painful. Simple things like making food feel like a chore if you flood your brain with too much dopamine before-hand. The reason this happens is that huge spikes in dopamine deplete the storage. When you engage in activities that are not as stimulating, your brain will release less dopamine than usual. If you manage to reduce your exposure to "supernormal stimuli", you will begin to find activities like making food, socializing, doing homework, reading and so on much more enjoyable.

Your capacity to feel pleasure and happiness is inversely proportional to how "overstimulated" your brain is. Gambling, binge-drinking, taking drugs, watching porn or watching hours of TV are examples of behavior that deplete your dopamine. I don't endorse living in a cave either, but my life has gotten much bet-ter without excess stimuli from personal experience. When you arrive home after work and find yourself bored, consider reading a book instead of watching TV. Consider listening to a podcast on the metro instead of browsing through memes or rubbish news. This is perhaps the best "trick" I can give you if you want to in-crease your quality of life in the long run. Choose your exposure to highly stimulating content wisely and if it doesn't add to your life, cut it out.

Your capacity to feel pleasure and happiness is inversely proportional to how "overstimulated" your brain is.

In the modern world, there are a lot of things we can get addicted to. To "stay free" these days, one must be strong and resilient. Homo Sapiens has been around for approximately 300 000 years. During this time, it is first after 2006 with the porn tube sites that porn has been very accessible. Some people experienced problematic porn use before this as well, but 2006 signaled a new era because of ease of access. This means that the "supernormal stimuli" of Internet porn has only been around for about 0,005 % of human history. Humans are mammals and mammalian evolution goes back approximately 200 million years! Human evolution is changing over time and Internet porn has already made a big impact on the younger generation.

Imagine what is going to happen in the future with more advanced content and technology. People might become un-interested in reproduction and prefer artificial stimuli instead. Technology is evolving rapidly, and society is becoming more re-liant upon it. In the future, it will probably be even more difficult to avoid heading down the slippery slope of Internet - and porn addiction. Plastic surgery, HD, various angles, anime and so on al-ready make porn highly stimulating, and as technology advances, it will become even worse. Many people prefer watching porn over sex with a partner. The scary thing is that this is already the case for a lot of people – probably millions, and I used to be one of them.

Many people prefer watching porn over sex with a partner. The scary thing is that this is already the case for a lot of people – probably millions, and I used to be one of them.

Sexual stimulation is the biggest natural dopamine hit we can experience. Many porn users are unable to reach orgasm with a partner (a common side effect of porn addiction). Others don't even find it particularly enjoyable to have sex. That is crazy. Hav-ing sex is perhaps the activity nature has programmed us to ex-perience the most pleasure from. If you don't find sex enjoyable, then what is going to make you feel good? This is a result of extreme overstimulation and porn is in many cases the biggest problem here.

For a person with a healthy reward circuit, dopamine is released in good amounts by doing things like performing well academically, in sports and social encounters. Constant sexual stimulation by watching porn will result in fewer incentives to reach natural rewards from other sources. People will consequently suffer financially, socially, academically – virtually in all aspects of their lives. Achieving something will not give the same dopamine release as it does in a healthy person. This explains how loss of motivation can occur from excessive porn use.

Nothing you do throughout your day will come close to the pleasure of viewing "the perfect porn scene". Suddenly, things you used to be passionate about, seem like chores. Before you know it, you stop playing the guitar, you stop playing soccer and you sit on the couch browsing through Facebook and you only take breaks now and then to watch porn. Do allow this to happen to yourself. And if it has, don't worry. In chapter 9, we will go through a comprehensive guide on how you can change this and start living your life.

KEY LESSONS

-       We have created "supernormal stimuli" such as porn. These stimuli can override naturally developed genetic pathways. This means that porn use can override our pathways linked to reproduction with other humans.

-       Watching porn gives instant pleasure. Finding a partner requires delayed gratification. This mismatch explains how porn use diminishes your ability and chance of finding a suitable partner.

-       Be conscious of the stimuli you allow in your life (TV, social media, etc.)

-       Sexual stimulation provides the biggest natural dopamine hit available. Too much self-imposed sexual stimulation will result in reduced incentives to reach rewards in other areas of your life. Your financial, academic and social success will suffer as a result.

CHAPTER 6: ADDICTION

SCIENCE BEHIND THE ADDICTION PROCESS

A protein called CREB is released when someone engages in addictive behavior. DeltaFosB (a transcription factor) promotes positive reinforcement of the given behavior. CREB is built up quickly in response to porn use, while DeltaFosB builds up slowly. This leaves the user vulnerable to relapse after discontinued use for long periods.

Watching Internet porn produces neuroplastic changes that reinforce the experience. These neuroplastic changes build new brain maps for sexual excitement. Previously established brain maps, like the natural process that is learned through thousands of years of evolution, is consequently weakened. The natural excitement process cannot compare to the new process. In the end, this can result in the individual seeking out even more graphic content online to maintain the same levels of excitement. This results in diminished interest in sex with a real partner.

Porn use desensitizes arousal. More hours spent watching porn per week results in lower gray matter volume in the right caudate of the brain. [30] Gray matter volume changes are correlated with multiple addictions. It is a region of the brain associated with sexual arousal and motivation. Gray matter is associated with decision-making, meaning that gray matter volume change alters our decision-making abilities. Left putaminal activity is reduced in response to porn after more hours. [30] This is responsible for the desensitization that occurs. Sexual arousal can furthermore reduce our ability to make calculated and wise decisions.

THE ADDICTION PROCESS

-       Pleasure chemicals are released in huge amounts.

-       The brain adjusts and starts to rely on greater stimuli to receive the same pleasure.

-       The brain rewires and seeks rewards through the new neural pathways that have been established.

Porn addiction resembles drug addiction. Brain changes observed in people with compulsive sexual behavior mirror those of drug addicts compared to controls. [31]

Our brains are the most complex organs in our bodies. It sits at the center for all human activity. The brain consists of billions of neurons (brain cells). Flow of information happens by neurons communicating with each other. The way this communication happens is by neurotransmitters being sent between neurons. Drugs can either release abnormally large amounts of neurotransmitters (n example is porn) or activate neurons because of chemical resemblance to neurotransmitters (an example is heroin).

THESE AREAS OF THE BRAIN ARE AFFECTED BY DRUG USE:

-       The extended amygdala - responsible for feelings of anxiety and unease associated with withdrawal.

-       The prefrontal cortex (PFC) - responsible for willpower and thinking ahead of time. Drug use weakens the PFC, which makes us more prone to look for instant gratification. The PFC is the last part of the brain to mature, meaning that early exposure to porn or drugs can have a detrimental effect on its development. This brain region is vital for many functions. Planning complex cognitive behavior, personality expression and making decisions are among them. After watching porn, the part of the PFC responsible for higher-level thinking and self-management is likely to regret consuming porn (if you try to quit). Feelings of despair, depression and lowered self-esteem can occur. The PFC can associate the withdrawal phase with increased stress. Binging is normal to escape unpleasant feelings.

- The basal ganglia - responsible for motivation and the reward circuit. Drugs reduce the sensitivity of this part of the brain through overstimulation.

Natural rewards produce fewer amounts of neurotransmitters than doing drugs. This means that continually taking drugs or watching porn will reduce your pleasure from natural activities since the big spikes will downregulate natural release from normal activities. Dopamine is naturally released when doing healthy behavior which activates our reward systems. Sexual behavior and drugs activate the same set of neurons within the same reward system structures. Simultaneously, very little overlap exists between other natural rewards, like food and addictive drugs. [32]

When huge amounts of dopamine are released as a response to drug use, this reinforces us to form a habit around it. The dopamine release teaches the brain that it should adapt and form a habit. Next, the brain adjusts by producing fewer neurotransmitters from natural reward or reduce the number of receptors that can receive transmitters.

KEY LESSONS

-        Porn use results in reduced interest and enjoyment from sex.

-        Porn use affects motivation, cognitive ability and social expression.

-        Sexual behavior and drugs activate the same neurons. Users commonly report reduced pleasure from everyday activities after prolonged porn use.

PART 2: BUILDING ON THE FOUNDATIONS

CHAPTER 7: WHO ARE YOU?

If you don't know what you want to achieve in your life, you are just a leaf in the wind. Many are like a jellyfish. They just float around with the current wherever it is convenient and easy to go. What you want to do instead is to find out exactly what you want out of life and go for it. The way to achieve this clarity is not commonly talked about. Most people never really find out what they want to achieve in their lives. As a result, they settle for what is expected of them. An ordinary life is great if that is what you truly want for yourself. Most people live comfortable and ordinary lives and the hardship required to forge a path in life is not present.

Great people achieve their success because they know what they want. You don't get to be president by accident. To do something great, you have to work hard for a long time. I think Arnold Schwarzenegger really makes the point. He didn't just show up randomly in Los Angeles in the 1960s and became Mr. Olympia by accident. Arnold wanted to become the best bodybuilder in the world so strongly that he was willing to do anything to get there. He made his entire life revolve around it. From sunrise to sunset, he spent all his time and energy on doing the things that would help him reach his goals. Then, he decided to pursue a career in acting and applied the same methodology. Then, he did the same thing in politics. He achieved tremendous success in these areas because of his work ethic. Before diving into a new thing, he locked in on the target with laser focus. In this chapter, you will find your values and goals. This will help you get out of bed early in the morning.

Most people that grow up in the Western world today have pretty comfortable lives. This is a good thing. In the Western world, safety nets for vulnerable people are provided. The result however, is that people don't have the same evolutionary pressure to go do something that people had historically.

If you were an apathetic little weakling in the 1800s, you would starve and die. Nowadays, a college dropout will most likely do just fine. His or her life will most likely be nothing compared to what it could have been, but it will still be okay. Consequently, most people lack the passion, drive and sheer willpower to make something great happen.

The objective of this chapter is to find our goals, values, rules and aspirations to live by. This is something that is commonly preached by various self-help gurus and motivational speakers. What they usually say is to just "find your goals". It sounds great, doesn't it? Just find your goals. Well, it is not as easy as it sounds. You have to sit down and expend a great deal of effort and do some "soul-searching" if you are going to get any closer to finding out what you truly value.

You might ask yourself: How is having life purpose going to help me quit porn? Good question. Well, when you have the clarity of knowing what you want, you will realize that you will have to say no to a lot of things to achieve it (if it is a massive goal). Porn has detrimental effects on your motivation, communication skills, focus and much more. We have covered this in exquisite detail in part 1 of this book. I hope you now understand why you should avoid it like the plague. Porn use affects our ability to work towards our goals.

If you have no goals in life, and your biggest aspiration is to simply feel pleasure, then why not watch porn 5 hours a day? Why not take up heroin? Doing drugs is perhaps the easiest way short-term to experience great pleasure. In the long run, excessive use of drugs, alcohol or porn is going to ensure a terrible life. What you need to do to live happily for years to come, is to take your future into account. Therefore, having a vision and path to follow is of the utmost importance. Without this all kinds of buffoonery and terrible things can happen to you.

MY STORY

Growing up I did well until about age 14. I had good grades, loyal friends and a good family. I lacked clarity on knowing what I wanted out of life though. Deep down, I knew I wanted to become successful at something, but I had so many interests that I found it difficult to pick something. I had interests ranging from sports to geography, travel, psychology, science, math, the universe and meditation. I had been socially anxious growing up, but it had been manageable. Then high school happened. I developed social anxiety and started having big issues with being around people. I sweated profusely, my face would turn red, I had difficulty making friends and couldn't express myself properly even around my family. As a result, my grades dropped significantly, and I got depressed. In this period, I started playing video games and watching porn to escape the weight of the world. I lost all my motivation and went into a downward spiral.

After high school, I decided to go to university to study structural engineering because it was expected of me. I couldn't handle it since my social anxiety persisted. Making new friends was impossible for me because I would be too nervous to communicate effectively. At this point, I realized that some of my problems could be related to porn addiction. I had some close friends that helped me through this period, and I am forever grateful for their support. After dropping out, I moved back home and started working as a truck driver. I hated this job and I could picture no future for myself. I almost didn't care if I lived or if I died because of social anxiety. This was the lowest point in my life. I couldn't see a path or way to get out. I can still vividly remember that I was frightened of menial things like going to the store. Writing about this today is fascinating because my life has turned around completely. I almost can't relate to the past, because my life has gotten so much better. For this reason, I feel obliged to share my story and the insights that helped me. You don't have to be at rock-bottom to benefit from these insights however, these principles can apply to anyone.

THE 3 GOLDEN RULES FOR FINDING PASSION ALONG THE WAY.

1. MOTION CREATES EMOTION.

If you currently don't know what to do with your life, this doesn't mean that you should sit on your ass, waiting for magic to happen. That is never going to happen. Only reading and doing research is not going to help you either. You must start acting through your interests or your fears. Doing this will give you a better understanding of what you want along the way. You probably have some interests already. Start working or take up hobbies that are in alignment with these interests. Motivation comes from action. It is not magically going to show up someday. Motivation is something that will increase as you try to forge a path. By doing something, you will get into a better mental state and suddenly, you experience glimpses of potential paths and added motivation.

2. USE FEAR AS A COMPASS.

Fear is an emotion that makes you try to avoid certain situations. Many people are overly anxious and afraid of things that are totally harmless these days. To expand as a person, going outside the comfort zone is required. Life starts outside your comfort zone. If you plan on doing anything of significance in your life, you must constantly step outside your comfort zone. Renewed passion and goals can often be found by engaging in challenging behavior. Your brain suddenly sees new possibilities that never came to mind before.

I consciously started working as a telemarketer to work on my social anxiety. In the beginning, it was stressful and challenging. After a while, I did well and developed a keen interest in communication and sales. Simultaneously, I managed to eradicate many of my fears. I decided to switch my workplace after a while and remember fearing eating lunch with my coworkers. 2 years later, I was awarded for outstanding performance multiple times. The funny thing was that I started in the worst position possible to succeed (being afraid to speak to people). Through persistence and hard work, I managed to climb to the top. I often think back to this if I think something is impossible or too difficult.

If you put your mind to it, your fears can eventually turn into your greatest gifts. If you don't go outside your comfort zone, you will stay the same, and staying the same when time passes by means declining. There is no such thing as remaining stagnant, you are either moving up or down.

3.   FIND MOTIVATION BASED ON DIFFERENT "LEVELS OF CONSCIOUSNESS".

The petty self may want to reach a goal to take revenge. Being in a bad mood, it is good to have something that motivates you. You probably have some neutral motivations as well. Things like become healthy, living a fulfilling life, having cool experiences and so on can be among them. Use this part of yourself to propel forward also. Finally, a part of you may want to achieve something in order to help other people and make a difference in the world.

The reason you want to have different "levels of motivation" is that depending on your mood and overall state, you will be triggered or resonate with different things. If you recently returned home from vacation and are well-rested, you may resonate with some of the higher-self motivations. If you are underslept, tired and angry, you probably resonate more with the petty motivations. There is nothing wrong with this. You just want to make sure that you work towards your goals no matter what. Use this insight in the "3 questions exercise".

ACHIEVE CLARITY BY KNOWING:

- What kind of person am I?

- What do I want to achieve in my life?

- Who are suitable friends and partners for that life?

The way I encourage you to achieve this clarity is to lock yourself away for 24 hours in a spot where your basic needs can be met without distractions. A bathroom is a perfect example. The point of the exercise is to reflect on these questions and write answers down. The answers are meant to guide your actions going forward. Please note that if a new life experience makes you reconsider, that is totally fine. The answers you write down are meant to be your "north star" going forward until new information presents itself.

If you do this exercise, you will pretty soon have more clarity than most people. It will provide the foundation for building a great life of your design. Answering the 3 questions will create a "magnetic field" that will automatically pull you away from porn. You will realize that porn is going to be detrimental to your mission. Answering the 3 questions is also going to make you more unreactive and self-centered. People or things can't distract you anymore.

SETTING GOALS THE RIGHT WAY

Goals are entirely subjective, but as a general guideline it is wise to base your goals on metrics that can be controlled. Becoming a great heart-surgeon is something you can do if you are committed. Becoming a celebrity is something that happens more by chance. So, as a rule of thumb: Set big goals but try to base them on controllable metrics.

Goals should be so inspiring that simply thinking about them gives you an energy boost. They should be so inspiring that you are willing to say no to a lot of things to achieve them. Look at the difference between these two health goals:

-        I want to lose 10 pounds.

-        I want to feel strong, healthy, energetic and have the energy to take care of my family in the best possible way.

Chances are that you feel a much bigger energy boost thinking about the second goal. Why? Because it is inspiring and reaching it will make your life tangibly better. The first goal feels more like a chore. Losing 10 pounds means that you will be in better shape. It is undoubtedly great if you manage to lose those love handles. The problem is that a goal like this may not provide enough motivation to power through inevitable hard times.

Grant Cardone interestingly explained this. He is a successful entrepreneur, motivational speaker and author. Until he was 25 years old though, he was a drug-addict and had very little to show for. Cardone shared an insight in an interview, which I think is highly applicable to overcoming porn use. He was addicted to drugs and tried to quit several times every day for a long period. Cardone went to rehab eventually. The workers at the treatment facility tried to make him content with only not using. Cardone kept in touch with his highest aspirations though. This is what he thinks helped him through it.

The problem with small-minded thinking is that if your only goal is to stay away from drugs or porn, why should you quit? Is it worth it to go through all the pain associated with quitting if the only result is a life without the substance with no other payoffs? Therefore, you must find a bigger reason than simply not watching porn or avoiding the negative effects of porn. The why must be so big that the period of initial suffering is well worth it in the long run. The reason is entirely subjective. If you set ordinary goals, it will be possible to reach them even with suboptimal habits. If your current goal is to hold on to your job and work out 3 times a week, this is something that can be done regardless of if you waste 20 hours a week watching porn or 40 hours a week watching Netflix. But if your main goal for the next year is to double your income, you couldn't waste as much time. Here are some examples that I have used personally:

-       I want to become the strongest version of myself possible.

-       I want to be there for my friends and family in the best possible way.

-       I want to obtain financial freedom.

-       I want to have a healthy relationship with a girl before 6 months.

-       I want to have a positive impact on the world.

-       I want to double my income in the next 12 months.

The problem with small-minded thinking is that if your only goal is to stay away from drugs or porn, then why should you quit? Is it worth it to go through all the pain associated with quitting if the only result is a life without the substance with no other payoffs than that?

You want to have a big goal pinned down in the future. To make sure you chip away at it, you want to separate it into smaller pieces. You should have intermediary goals to build momentum. Managing to stick to the small goals is going to give you added motivation and self-confidence. This will make it more likely that you reach the big, big goals. Write down intermediary goals also when answering the 3 questions.

Goals should be specific, with a time limit. Otherwise, why should you start now? Why not wait until tomorrow? For this reason, there should always be a time limit and a specific out-come in mind, whether it is money or something else. If you don't reach the end goal, but you manage to reach many intermediary goals leading to that big goal, you will go far either way.

STOICISM

Stoicism is an ancient Greek philosophy. Perhaps its most important teaching is that we can't control or rely on external events, only ourselves and our responses. I think it is important when setting goals, that we base them upon things we can control. For example, if you go out to try to meet new people, be happy that you had the guts to approach. Don't base your self-respect on other people's reactions or opinions. Base it on your values and if you live up to them or not. There will always be problems in your life, no matter what. But make a commitment to yourself of staying happy and content either way.

> *"Let us prepare our minds as if we'd come to the very end of life. Let us postpone nothing. Let us balance life's books each day. … The one who puts the finishing touches on their life each day is never short of time."* – Seneca

Meditating on your mortality is only painful if you miss the point of it. The reason this can be a good exercise is that you will understand the shortness of your life. It will be obvious that you should not squander any more time. Keeping this in mind when you do the exercise, will make you a little uncomfortable if you lock yourself away for 24 hours, but it will make you value your time more in the aftermath.

THE EXERCISE:

Lock yourself away for 24 hours, schedule it in your calendar. Some circumstances can make this impossible or difficult for some people. If so, in the very least use 1 hour to think through the 3 questions and make notes on the answers.

1.   WHAT KIND OF PERSON AM I?

What are my strengths and weaknesses? What are my core values and ideals, and do I live in alignment with them? How do I relate to other people? How do other people view me? What are my deepest desires and motivations? What are my morals? What is acceptable behavior and what is not acceptable? What do I admire? How does the world work?

2.   WHAT KIND OF LIFE DO I WANT TO LIVE?

Make this as detailed as possible: devices, vehicle, home, travel, food, friends, romantic partners, work situation, financial situation, personality, impact on other people. What kind of career do I want? What kind of social life do I want? What do I want to expend my energy and focus on? What kind of habits and health do I want? How will I feel if I fail to secure the life I want? How do I want to feel?

3.   WHO WOULD BE GREAT COMPANIONS FOR THIS LIFE?

What kind of benefits am I capable of providing to other people? What kind of friends do I want to surround myself with and what kind of personality and skills should they have? What kind of romantic partner(s) do I want? How do I want to relate to other people? Should I focus most of my attention on a specific type of person? What kind of people should I avoid? How will my life turn out if I fail to secure the alliances I want?

FURTHER REFLECTIONS ON THE 3 QUESTIONS

If you are a recovering alcoholic, it will be in your best interest to avoid people that drink. This way, you don't have to withstand peer-pressure continually. For the people that enjoy alcohol, it is probably not going to be a fun time to be around you either. Your differing stance will challenge them. The same concept applies to any value that you feel strongly about. It will be beneficial for yourself and your comrades if you find people with shared goals and values. You will then be able to grow together and help each other along the way.

If you fail to answer the 3 questions, you will continually be pulled in different directions. You will suffer if you never find your core values are. The human equivalent of a jellyfish is perhaps the best description. Keep the old saying that you are the average of the 5 people you surround yourself with the most in mind. Simultaneously, it is impossible to find people that we have a 100 % overlap in personality with. It can be a great thing to allow conflicting ideas and points of view into our lives. There are many roads to Rome. Try to generally be around people trying to walk the same path as yourself. If you have different views on how to reach those goals, that is great.

Imagine that you are the CEO of a tampon company. You are responsible for the marketing budget. Do you want to market yourself to men or women? I hope your answer to that question is women. Now, are women of any age interested in your product? Well, only those of reproductive age presumably. Next, you may have to take a few more swipes at it, and for economic reasons or distributional reasons, you probably get rid of even more. In the end, perhaps 5 % of the population is interested in your product. Should you market yourself to everyone or just the 5 % that can potentially be profitable customers? Obviously, it would be better financial management to market towards that 5 %. You might ask yourself: Well, how does this apply to my choice of friends and partners? If you know what you really value in a person, you can actively seek out these characteristics and both your life and your new friend will be able to grow together.

Answering the 3 questions is of the utmost impo will help you seek out the people you should be around ᴜᴀᴛ ᴡ... steer you towards your goals instead of away from them.

CURRENT FRIENDS

A common occurrence for the ones that partake in this challenge, is that they will realize that many of the people they currently associate with are not heading down the same path as themselves. You shouldn't call your friends and end the friendship with them straight away though. What you want to do, is to seek out new people that embody your values and continually expand your social circle until most are going on a shared mission. This is a gradual process, and not something that can be achieved overnight. This is important to understand. If someone doesn't match your goals and values but has contributed greatly to your life before, you want to keep that person around. Real friends are hard to find. Acquaintances you don't share values with should be cut off. Before you know it, you are surrounded by people that want to help each other achieve shared goals.

Befriend high-quality people by being useful. Give them value and some will become your new friend. You shouldn't look at this as a value exchange, but a healthy and organic relationship. Give first, but don't expect anything in return. Some of the people you make yourself useful to will reciprocate, others will not and that is life. How can I make myself more useful to others? Adopt this mindset. Before you know it, you will have new high-quality friends and you will have the power of choosing who you want to spend your time with.

WHAT TO DO AFTER THE 3 QUESTIONS EXERCISE? REFLECTIONS ON CONFIDENCE

What is confidence? Confidence is commonly described as

a belief in oneself. Being sure of yourself and your abilities is another definition. Many people believe confidence is something you are born with or without. Others believe it can be trained. I believe it is a highly trainable attribute. Confidence basically means your level of trust in yourself. There is one way to build real confidence. It is to build a track record of following through on your commitments. Simply being aware of this can change everything.

Confidence is not something you can magically sort out in your head. While struggling with social anxiety, I was often told just to be confident. It doesn't work like this. Integrity is the degree to which you follow your values and morals. Your brain keeps track of how much you live up to your values and promises. In your peer group, everyone knows who is trustworthy and who is not. The same thing happens within your brain. How much trust you have in yourself is based on the tally your brain keeps, and this is reflected externally as confidence.

There is one way to build real confidence. It is to build a track record of following through on your commitments.

How often do you follow through on the things that you decide to do? All the time? Most of the time? Sometimes? If you do what you are supposed to do every time, you should definitely trust yourself. If you never follow through, then no wonder you do not lead well. This is going to reflect on how others perceive you as well. For this reason, I encourage you to be reluctant to make commitments, but finish what you commit to! If you decide to make dinner after work but feel a little tired, do it anyway.

Continually setting small tasks and commitments and following through will make your confidence skyrocket in no time. Become such a good executor by incorporating this concept in your life, that your friends think you are dead if you fail to show up for something! When you decide to do something, following through is in your selfish best interest. You need to be able to trust yourself if you want to do something significant. And if you don't trust yourself, how are others going to be able to trust you? How can a spouse trust you as a life partner if you don't trust yourself? Whatever you aspire to do or want to achieve in your life, having confidence is extremely vital. Make commitments and follow through!

Men generally build self-esteem by taking action. Failure to take action results in less confidence and a need for approval from the environment. On the other hand, women constantly pay off the environment to feel confident. They need constant reassurance that everything will be okay. This is perhaps the main difference between male and female psychology. Women want a man that is secure in himself and resourceful since they commonly lack the sense of security within themselves. Avoiding porn or doing nofap are great ways to build confidence for men since it requires building discipline and doing something proactively. Men that don't have the balls to take action still crave certainty. Nice guys try to experience certainty through communication. These men rely on approval from friends and social validation to feel certainty. Don't allow yourself to be that guy. Do what you are supposed to do (we all know this deep down) and you will communicate certainty by default. This will make women attracted as well.

SOCIAL PROOF

The concept of social pressure is a tendency that affects everyone to various degrees. One issue frequently comes up when you know how to go forward after doing the 3 questions exercise. What we want to do is very individual. Your goals and values in life probably can't be placed in a box. We normally have some values that align with some groups of people, and others commonly held by completely different types of people.

We are unique human beings. This means that we will face social pressure if we live in alignment with our values. The best way to practice this is to be firm and trust yourself. Sometimes it is going to be uncomfortable. If you believe something, hold on to your belief regardless of how others view the matter. If you feel like someone is taking advantage of you, speak up. Dare to speak your mind and let people know when they cross your boundaries. If you do this consistently, you will be able to live a life completely of your design. When you define your values, some people will try to challenge you. You have to be able to handle some conflict. How can you go for what you really want as a unique person, if you allow people's opinions to affect you and your actions?

TAKING ACTION

When you know what you value, you should try to spend your time almost exclusively on activities that bring you closer to your goals. If watching TV shows is not something you value, you should probably use your time on something else. This doesn't mean that you should become egocentric though. If you value friendships and loyalty, compromise is sometimes required.

When you know which principles to live by, you can derive happiness from within if you manage to live in alignment with them. It is vital to find your values, and not blindly follow groupthink. If you don't take the time to think through what you really value, you might never live congruently. That is scary, much scarier than having to withstand some social pressure now and then. The risky thing is never finding out who you really are.

You are the average of the 5 people you surround yourself with the most. You have probably heard this somewhere before. Well, science can actually back up this claim. Willpower, bad habits and positive change spreads between people almost like germs. If your friend becomes obese, your risk of becoming obese increases by 171 %. [33] This shows the importance of whom you hang out with. If you and your friends have different aspirations and goals, you are not in an optimal spot. If you and your friends have similar aspirations and goals, you will grow together.

We all have something called mirror neurons. These brain cells' function is to observe and keep track of other people's feelings. Contagion of emotion and mimicking behavior are the by-products of mirror neurons.

Here is an example you can probably relate to. Imagine it is Thursday evening and you have a morning shift at work 7 am tomorrow. You are enjoying the evening with a close friend at an exclusive restaurant. Your friend orders a couple of beers. You told yourself beforehand that you wouldn't drink tonight. Before you know it, you have gulped several beers. You wake up the next morning and arrive late to work because that one drink turned into a few. Having a drink is not necessarily a bad thing. Still, mirror neurons empathize with other people's decisions, which make you more susceptible to behave similarly – whether it is good or bad behavior. This means that if you manage to build a peer-group with high-quality people, your mirror neurons will mimic their high-quality behavior. On the other hand, if you are surrounded by buffoons, you will be affected negatively.

You should be very careful about whom you spend your time with. If your friends have different goals and values from you, you are not setting yourself up for success. Goal contagion is a real thing. If you find yourself being around people that have conflicting goals with you temporarily, it is possible to some-what reduce this effect by "vaccinating" yourself. If you often think about your goals and are very aware of them, simply seeing someone doing the opposite will not throw you off balance. This ensures that you are not a leaf in the wind that responds to random circumstances.

The importance of having a "hero" or someone to look up to, is also not to be neglected. When you face a challenge, you can ask yourself what your hero would do in this situation. This makes it more likely that you will face a challenge head-on and perhaps go for the harder choice, which will be the best option long-term. People that have faced the same challenges as you and managed to overcome them provide great motivation.

If you have done the 3 questions exercise by now, con-gratulations! If not, go back and schedule at least 1 hour to think through your life going forward!

KEY LESSONS

-       Lock yourself away in a place where your basic needs can be met (like a bathroom) for 24 hours to answer the 3 questions. 1: What kind of person am I? 2: What kind of life do I want? 3: Who would be good companions for that life? If you don't have the time, reflect for 1 hour and write down the answers.

-       Without knowing what you want out of life, you are the human equivalent of a jellyfish. You just go with the flow. Other people's opinions will guide your actions instead of your inner maps.

-       Motivation comes from action. It does not come from sitting on your ass, waiting for something to happen. Use fear as a compass to start taking action.

-       Set big goals for the future and separate them into smaller, manageable parts.

-       Seek out new friends that align with your goals and values. Make yourself useful to other high-quality people. This is the best and easiest way to befriend them.

-       Confidence comes from building a track-record of following through on your commitments.

-       The ability to tolerate social pressure is extremely vital if you want to live in alignment with your values. There is inevitably going to be some friction and in order to not give in, you have to be able to handle some conflict.

CHAPTER 8: PERSPECTIVE

It is a modern-day luxury to be a soft weakling. It has never been easier to live than it is for people in the western world today. Still, many people face grueling life circumstances in parts of Africa and Asia. There is a lack of drinking water and people die from various diseases. This is not meant to depress you. Not everyone has the luxury to watch Internet porn compulsively or waste their lives procrastinating.

Porn can cause massive issues in people's lives but compared to the things our ancestors had to go through, it is nothing. The fact that you can afford this book, puts you in a demographic of people with tremendous opportunities. Today, things like jets are available and you can fly across the world rather inexpensively. We should be tremendously grateful for what we have. Our ancestors died with tears in their eyes, wishing they could have the opportunities now available. Don't squander your life, lying around doing not much. With a lack of food and scarcity, people had to work hard for survival previously. If you manage to adopt only a fraction of the hustle people had back in the day, you will become successful very fast. The competition is sleeping. Stop caring about your short-term emotions, care about your long-term outcomes.

A mere mortal today has more power through their smartphone than kings had historically. By clicking some buttons, they bring you food. They pick you up with an Uber after pressing a couple of buttons. They fly you across the world after a few swipes and clicks. This is fantastic and gives us power no one has ever had in history. At the same time, with a device this powerful in our hands, it is easy to become soft and lazy.

Michael Phelps is the most decorated Olympic athlete of all time. He has won as much as 23 Olympic gold medals. To achieve this feat, he had to engage in extreme behaviors. Phelps' training regimen consisted of swimming for hours every day, for many years. He also lifted weights for an hour and stretched for an hour 3 days per week. To have exceptional outcomes, one must engage in exceptional behaviors. Only fools or people that spend way too much money on lottery tickets expect otherwise. Success comes from sacrificing the moment for a bigger picture goal in the future. For Michael Phelps, this meant swimming hours every day, whether he felt like it or not. Some days he was probably content and enjoyed swimming. Other days, he probably just wanted to relax.

When you go do the thing regardless of your emotions, a beautiful shift happens. When you don't feel like doing something is the time you will build your willpower the most. If you manage to make a track record of following through on your commitments regardless of your short-term emotions, magic will happen. If you know that you are going to do the thing anyway, why not make the most of it? Why not feel as happy and content as humanly possible, if you know that you are going to do the thing anyway?

This concept can be applied to things like nutritional habits, working out, studying or simply learning any new skill. If someone decides to start lifting weights after having been a couch potato their entire life, it will probably suck the first month. They will be mentally exhausted and physically drained at first. After a while, their body will begin to adjust. If they don't give up during the first couple of months and continue the training regimen, their body will adapt. Results will follow quickly. Avoiding porn is similar. The first month or so is difficult, but after a while our brain adjusts and suddenly it is rather effortless to avoid porn. This is also the reason I have included exercises for strengthening willpower in this manual. Willpower is required to go through the initial phase of quitting.

WHAT THE CLASSIC "THE HUSTLER" BY WALTER TEVIS, CAN TEACH US ABOUT SUCCESS

In the famous novel, Tevis describes a young pool player called Eddie Felson, who is one of the best in business. He dives deep down into the hidden dynamics that determine winners from losers. Tevis says that it is much harder to win than to lose. Felson was a great pool player, but he didn't have the mental stamina and wisdom required to win. So, every time he built a bankroll, he would squander it.

If you want to win consistently, you have to keep a level head when you make mistakes. You don't want to start taking the pressure off by complaining. Imagine that you are trailing behind in a contest and chances are looking slim. When things seem difficult, it is very easy to complain and blame various circumstances. Yeah, I know, you were unlucky, or you didn't get enough sleep last night. It is much harder to keep your head down and continue your a-game when you know that chances are slim. This is what is required if you want to be a consistent winner in life. People that have played sports or excelled in any competition can attest to this.

Complaining and making excuses is a way of telling yourself it is okay to lose. It makes losing more bearable. Losing if you have a winning mindset is painful, but if you manage to stick to the champion mindset and continue to look for ways to improve, you will get better. This concept is highly applicable to avoiding porn and many other pursuits as well. It is easy to blame others or make excuses, but it is only by taking responsibility we can learn from your mistakes.

Every time you catch yourself being annoyed or angry with something, consider it a call to action. If you find yourself complaining about something, it means you have failed to act. I use this as a mental note. If I complain or my mood is down for some reason, it means I have failed to do what I was supposed to do and fix it as soon as possible. Some things are outside our control, like the weather. Avoid overthinking stuff that is outside your control. But if your boss mistreats you or you are disappointed in yourself from failing to do something, fix it! Tell your boss or co-worker what you think. Do it in a calibrated way though, so you don't get fired. Adopt this mental rule and your life will for the better never be the same; complaints signal that it is time to act.

Adopt this mental rule and your life will for the better

never be the same; complaints signal that it is time to act.

KEY LESSONS

-       We have opportunities today that our ancestors could have killed for. Use these opportunities!

-       To have excellent outcomes, one must engage in exceptional behaviors.

-       When adopting a new habit, the initial phase will be painful, but if you stick to it, your body will adapt, and it will be much easier to do the thing eventually.

-       To excel you have to learn from your mistakes. View mistakes as learning opportunities, not a failure.

-       If you complain, it means that you need to resolve an issue.

CHAPTER 9: HOW TO TAKE CONSCIOUS CONTROL OF YOUR HABITS

This advice is not meant to substitute professional help. Consider seeking professional help from a therapist.

In this book, we have so far looked at avoiding porn and not really covered masturbation as much. Many try to avoid masturbation when they quit watching porn. I do nofap, which means that I only climax with a partner. I don't masturbate. Medical research indicates that it could be healthy though to masturbate occasionally. It suggests that sexual stimulation by masturbation can:

- Elevate mood

- Enhance your quality of sleep

- Reduce stress

- Release tension

- Reduce the risk of prostate cancer for men [34]

These benefits occur short-term. If you live a life of your design aligned with your values, you will not accumulate much distress throughout the day. If you go out and slay dragons every day, your mood will not need temporary elevation. Masturbation when you are on a mission, will only distract you and sap your energy. Fix the root cause, don't medicate the problem. If you experience trouble sleeping, tension or distress, something in your life needs to be redesigned. Drinking too much, watching porn, excessive masturbation and doing drugs are common ways of self-medicating an existence that should be changed. Distress and complaints are calls to action, meaning something should be changed.

A famous study has pointed out that if a man doesn't masturbate, his testosterone increases to 145,7 % of the baseline the seventh day. [35] Testosterone is a very important hormone for men, responsible for sex drive, motivation, energy and many other vital functions. Sperm is the most capital-intensive tissue the body produces, and excessive masturbation can be unhealthy because it can lower testosterone levels.

Prolactin is a hormone that is released after climax to combat the depressing effect that overuse of the dopamine system has. After sex, much higher levels of prolactin are released than after masturbation (for men). This can explain why some people feel down after masturbation. I have more energy, focus, willpower and motivation if I don't jerk off. This may not be the case for everyone, but many find that avoiding porn is easier if nofap is done simultaneously. Jerking off is not the worst thing you can do; porn is the biggest danger.

Perhaps the biggest reason people struggle with addiction or unwanted behavior, is that their current lifestyle is unable to provide enough satisfaction to feel content or happy. Relationships are universally ranked as the most important part of people's lives. [36] It is here people experience most of their happiness and good emotions.

Many become addicted to porn or other things because they lack meaningful relationships. This can be because they have various problems that reduce their ability to build good relationships. Issues like social anxiety, poor social skills, general anxiety and shyness can contribute to this. It is very important for people that struggle to connect with others, to build their social skills while trying to quit porn. If you manage to power through and quit porn temporarily, but you are unable to build better relationships, you likely won't be able to maintain success.

Addiction is often a coping strategy. Problematic porn use is for many a result of a lack of meaningful relationships. On one hand, it can be very difficult to build relationships while watching too much porn as it turns many into "zombies" that have little interest in socializing. Simultaneously, if we take away the pleasure of porn with no substitute, many feel lonely very fast. For this reason, build your social skills while trying to quit! Go out there and meet new people.

REFLECTIONS ON PAIN

Pain will inevitably show up when trying to quit porn or do nofap. Strengthening your willpower and saying no to temptation is difficult. It is preferable to the alternative, which is pain coming from disappointment and not living up to your full potential. You can choose pain proactively in the short-term by building your willpower and denying yourself the pleasure of porn, or you can choose pain in the future - which will be much worse when you realize what could have been. Realizing that your life is nothing compared to what it could have been, is not a fun experience. I don't endorse that at all.

> *You can choose pain proactively in the short-term by building your willpower and denying yourself the pleasure of porn, or you can choose pain in the future - which will be much worse when you realize what could have been.*

Choose pain in the short-term proactively by doing the right thing. The right thing is not always easy. Your future self will thank you, and you will experience less pain overall. The difference is that you have to choose it now for yourself instead of having it bite you in the ass in the future. Failing to accept this and not proactively building your discipline is like going into the hood and taking up a loan with huge interests that compounds into 100s of percent annually. Don't take up that loan!

We obviously don't like pain. We are willing to go great lengths to avoid it. The problem is that pain is practically inevitable. Since we don't like it, we have aversions to choose it proactively.

Working out really makes the example. Unfit people have big issues sticking to it in the beginning. They experience self-inflicted pain when they decide to leave the sofa for the first time. Well, what happens if they decide to stay a couch-potato, and deny the proactive, temporary pain? Heart disease, obesity, cardiovascular problems and a lot of other things can happen. They might die earlier if they never begin working out. They decide to stay less attractive than they could have been. As you can see, all kinds of pain will gradually show up if someone decides to avoid pain in the short-term. Accept this sooner rather than later.

A beautiful shift will begin to happen if you take on difficult challenges and stick with them. After a while your brain and body adjust and before you know it, working out is not unbearable. It can actually make you feel good! For this to resonate with you, you must start taking your future self into account. Most people don't have a concept of self, more than 6 months into the future. Try to circumvent this by laying plans that go further ahead. Doing this will change your outlook on what matters. For example, would you choose to have one difficult year ahead if you knew the following 50 would be amazing? Most people would take that deal, given the option. Lack of perspective ensures that the next 50 will be mediocre at best.

Champion behavior requires you to neglect your emotions in the short-term. Start taking your future self into account. Don't be a dick to him or her. The more real your future self feels to you, the easier it will be to make decisions right now you won't regret later.

 ## TRICKS AND HABITS THAT WILL MAKE IT EASIER FOR YOU TO AVOID PORN:

- REDUCE SCREEN TIME

Reduce the time spent on social media or your cell phone/ computer in general. If you want to read or research something, try to purchase hardcover books whenever possible. The Internet is one of the best inventions ever created. The flip side is that it is highly addictive. It can be used for both good and bad. For some people, it can be a good idea to delete social media accounts, at least temporarily. This will ensure that the digital presence is reduced to a bare minimum for a period.

The most sustainable approach in my opinion, is to maintain a digital presence on social media etc., but keep the use limited and conscious. If you manage to control your social media use, you are in a much better position to control your porn habits. If you can't control your use of social media, how can you control more intense porn urges? As soon as you find yourself mindlessly searching the web or doing any kind of mindless behavior, stop and do something else. If you have answered the 3 questions, you know what to do immediately.

- AVOID UNNECESSARY STIMULI.

This can be things like browsing Instagram, reading online newspapers filled with graphic images, browsing Facebook mindlessly and staring at posters of lightly dressed people. Avoid any kind of series or movies where nakedness is abundant. You don't have to do this for the rest of your life, but avoiding it for a period can be very helpful. Today, a lot of TV-shows and movies are filled with softcore porn. Watch this at your own peril. If you want to quit porn, this is a sacrifice that can help you.

- ACCOUNTABILITY!

Accountability helps tremendously. Reach out to like-minded people and connect with them. A team is always stronger than someone going solo. You can learn from each other as well. This is huge.

- NEVER BRING YOUR DEVICES INTO BED.

- BREATHING.

One way to boost your willpower immediately is to slow down your breathing pattern to about 4-6 breaths per minute. After having done this technique for a few minutes, you will feel calm and collected and find yourself in control. This is very helpful if you experience strong urges. Becoming present kills urges. Allowing yourself to feel the urge before you go do something will build self-control rapidly. After staying with the feeling for a while, it usually goes away. If you continually try to distract yourself as soon as a craving appears, you will not learn how to deal with the craving head-on. Allowing yourself to stay with the feeling for a few moments will make you stronger very fast.

- PLAN FOR A WORST-CASE SCENARIO.

Imagine that you are feeling bad and are about to give in. You are lying in bed contemplating visiting some websites you know you should not visit. What does it feel like? What steps should you take to avoid the relapse? Go outside and have some fresh air perhaps? How does this feel? Visualizing and preparing for a scenario like this help when you have successfully abstained for a few days or more. This scenario will most likely happen. If you have visualized it and prepared yourself mentally beforehand, you will probably be able to execute the right way in real-time.

- DELAY.

Put a delay or roadblock between your feelings of temptation and your ability to act on them. One of the things that makes it so difficult to stop watching porn, is its ease of access. It can be wise to install blockers so that you can't access content from your Wi-Fi. Plenty of other solutions are available, be creative!

- BE MORE SOCIAL.

Make sure you spend a lot of time in public. If you spend a lot of time in social environments, you will feel evolutionary pressure to adapt. If you watch porn 3 hours a day, you will be walking around like a zombie, and have trouble being normal in social encounters. If you force yourself to be in social environments constantly, you will have added leverage to quit. Use the time you would have spent on your computer, out there in the real world. Replace bad habits with good ones.

GENERAL HABITS TO ENGAGE IN:

- HAVE A PLAN FOR THE NEXT DAY.

For me, this was extremely important. If you know what you are supposed to do the next day, waking up late and wasting hours on the Internet is not going to happen. If you have no plan and structure for the day, you can suddenly find that you have wasted hours. Before you know it, you find yourself browsing various porn tabs out of boredom and guilt. To avoid this, make a habit of having a plan or idea of what you want to do the next day.

I remember when starting on my journey of recovery, that it was very painful to endure weekends with minimal social contact. I started reading books, working out and going for walks. When I threw away the crutch of porn, I had to go through a few lonely weekends. A couple of months later, I had new friends to hang out with. If you complete the exercise with the 3 questions, you will know what to do.

- CHIP AWAY AT YOUR GOALS EVERY SINGLE DAY.

The temporary satisfaction you receive from watching porn or TV is nothing compared to the lasting and inner satisfaction that can be achieved by applying yourself and staying on the grind. This is how you build self-respect and confidence. If you continually chip away at your goals, the inner satisfaction and happiness you obtain will help guide you away from porn. Normally, relapses happen at low points. It is less likely you will find yourself in a bad mood if you do something every day to make your future better.

-       "DOPAMINIZE" YOUR LEAST FAVORITE TASKS.

For example: After completing a workout, give yourself a treat or listen to your favorite podcast while making dinner. Although this trick can be a nice way to get things done, don't always use it – use it when you need a little extra motivation to get something done. You want to have activities and periods of your day when you get used to having no artificial stimuli. This will make other activities more enjoyable.

-       CREATE ALGORITHMS FOR THE PROCESSES IN YOUR LIFE.

This will ensure that you don't spend time and mental energy every day, trying to reinvent the wheel. An example of this can simply be using a morning routine. For example: Go out of bed into the shower immediately after waking up. Make yourself a cup of coffee/tea. Eat. Meditate for 10 minutes. If you manage to create useful algorithms for a few healthy habits like this, it can make a big difference and you will become more effective. It can also help you build focus and discipline, which is crucial to stay away from porn effectively.

-       STRENGTHEN YOUR WILLPOWER.

Every time you have the option to work on your willpower, do it! You don't get to work on your willpower at a time when it is convenient. You only get to work on your willpower, when there is something you don't feel like doing. If you are tired, underslept or stressed out from work, it is an excellent opportunity to work on your willpower. Although it might not be good for your body in the long run to constantly work out if you are fatigued, doing it on occasion will strengthen your willpower. If you are not currently strong enough to control your porn or masturbation habits, start with a smaller self-control act. You can build a lot more strength rapidly if you try to increase the difficulty of your practices. Think of it like you are a mental athlete. Try to go further and further in your self-control endeavors. Before you know it, you are a firm executor leaving others trailing behind.

-       REMOVE UNNECESSARY USE OF WILLPOWER.

Willpower is like a muscle. If you remove temptations, you will have more willpower left when it really matters! Things like removing notifications on social media, removing candy bowls etc. will ensure that you stay strong for the moments that matter. We make tremendous amounts of decisions every day regarding food. If we reduce some of them, we have more willpower at our disposal to focus on other things like avoiding porn, doing nofap, working out or doing homework.

-       TRANSMUTE SEXUAL ENERGY.

Whenever you experience arousal or feel like caving in, transmute that energy into something productive - like working out. Simply doing some pushups, going for a walk or going to the gym will alleviate some pent-up energy and make you more relaxed afterward. If you feel really aroused and you don't have a partner, transmute that energy into something productive! This is why finding new hobbies when trying to quit porn is of the utmost importance. If we fail to transmute our newfound energy into something else, it will be very difficult to change permanently. Find new things to use your time on. Stay productive!

REFLECTIONS ON DOPAMINE CRAVINGS

Most of us go into states at times we feel like we "need" dopamine hits. If you are tired and stressed out, pulling out your cell phone to check social media is the easy way out. Just waiting a few seconds can be painful in this state. In these situations, my best recommendation is to calm down and stay with the uneasy feeling. If you manage to stay present (it is uncomfortable) in a state where you crave dopamine, you will feel more relaxed after a while. This is the way you will be able to quit porn as well.

You have to train yourself to tolerate these cravings when they occur. Before you know it, life in itself will bring you enough joy. Suddenly, you don't have to rely on the stimuli provided by a screen. The next time you find yourself on the bus, take a look around. Most are slaves to their cell phones. Sit there and enjoy the view instead. It will be much more fulfilling to stay present in the long run than constantly looking for the next dopamine hit like a junkie on social media. Try to become consciously aware of this and practice it for the rest of your life.

Here I have outlined a 7-week program. Follow this program to the best of your ability. Engage in the habits every day.

THE PROGRAM

WEEK 1-2:

Quit porn

Read for at least 20 minutes every day (physical book)

Conscious Internet use

Go to the gym at least 3 days a week

WEEK 3-4:

Quit porn

Read for at least 20 minutes every day (physical book)

Conscious Internet use

Go to the gym at least 3 days a week

Cold showers

WEEK 5-6:

Quit porn

Read for at least 20 minutes every day (physical book)

Conscious Internet use

Go to the gym at least 3 days a week

Cold showers

Meditation 15 minutes every day

WEEK 7-8:

Quit porn

Read for at least 20 minutes every day (physical book)

Conscious Internet use

Go to the gym at least 3 days a week

Cold showers

Meditation 15 minutes every day

Challenging social encounter every day

FURTHER REFLECTIONS

If you manage to implement the habits and feel like you need more challenges, you can try to implement them faster than suggested.

Many people that try to quit porn reach for 90 days. That is a good target. The ideal situation though, is to go on indefinitely. This program lasts for 8 weeks, which is 56 days. If you successfully make it through, try to go further. It takes a while before the brain rewires, especially if the addiction started at an early age. Progress can normally be noticed pretty early. Social encounters feel more natural already after a few days without porn.

Research is not entirely accurate on how long it takes before habits are ingrained. Some claim that it takes 21 days. Repetition is vital to make sure that habits stick. Most of us are not good multitaskers. It is important to build positive reinforcement by sticking to what you commit to. If you manage to read for 20 minutes a day for 2 weeks, it will become easier as time goes by to continue the habit. Once a new habit is established, it is much easier to take on a new one. When you manage to build good habits and you stay consistent, it is often more painful to not do the thing after a while than to do it.

A person that has worked out consistently for a long time will feel like something bad is happening if they are not allowed to go to the gym. Become like that! Your life is holistic, which means that what you do in one area of your life, will affect the rest. If you use your spare time doing things that make yourself proud, chances are it will affect your career positively and vice versa. Doing well in one area is going to affect the rest of your life positively. Watching random people copulate online is going to do exactly the opposite.

READING

Reading for 20 minutes a day will build focus and discipline. For a normal person, discipline is required to read, since we are so used to stimulation. Our average attention span has short-ened dramatically in the last decades. Do this without checking your cell phone, only focus on reading, preferably a hardcover book.

DIGITAL USE

If you manage to use the Internet completely consciously for the rest of your life, you will not relapse to Internet porn ever again. Think about that for a second. To avoid porn, you need to control your Internet habits. Therefore, a great way to start is to take conscious control of social media use. Don't allow your mind to wander and search mindlessly for unnecessary things. Try to do this every day for the rest of your life.

If you manage to use the Internet completely consciously for the rest of your life, you will never relapse to Internet porn again!

The Internet is a fantastic tool for staying in touch with people, learning etc. but don't let it run you. Use it proactively, but as soon as you find yourself doing mindless things, stop immediately.

Some of the greatest minds of our time are trying to figure out how they can make people more addicted to their cell phones. You can't watch porn unless you are using your cellphone or personal computer, in most cases. By reducing the time spent on these devices and being conscious when using them, you will reduce the likelihood of relapsing. Most of the news we are exposed to provoke either a neutral or negative response. It is basically only sapping our energy.

The most successful people in the world understand that their focus is limited. They can't afford to be exposed to digital garbage since it will only distract them from the important things they have to do. I suggest you do the same. Your time is just as valuable as theirs, you probably just don't realize it. You are living your life, not someone else's.

Time is our most precious resource. Our time is limited, and everybody has 24 hours in their day regardless of how successful they are. Companies like Facebook and YouTube capitalize on stealing our attention. They basically benefit from our weaknesses. They earn more money, the more distracted we get from our real lives. These sites mostly provide temporary illusionary joy. It is in their best interest that you waste your time scrolling through endless tabs of half-naked models. Sean Parker served as the first president of Facebook. He has admitted that the social network was intended to distract, not unite us. By exploiting weaknesses in human psychology, Facebook and similar companies manage to capitalize by literally stealing people's most precious commodity; their time.

With all the stimuli and distractions that are available these days, many are losing control. Becoming strong enough to resist temptation is the best answer to it. When control is regained, you can choose what you want to use your time on. If you want to succeed in the world, having the ability to focus is extremely important. When the competition is sleeping and browsing through Facebook, you can use that time productively and gain an advantage. It is perhaps the best gift you as an individual can get, that most people aren't serious. If you are serious about your outcomes in life, you will look awesome by comparison in no time.

EXERCISES TO BUILD SELF-CONTROL:

- RESTRICT DIGITAL USE

The last hour before going to sleep, do not use any electronic devices. Use this time around family, a book or something else. If you manage to do this every single day, you will be in a great position to avoid porn entirely as well. For half an hour after waking up in the morning, don't use your devices either. This means that you have to buy an alarm clock, but this is a small sacrifice to make. Most of us immediately reach for our cell phones when we wake up, and are instantly triggered by news, notifications and so on. It is easy to lose track of what is important. Spending time every morning by yourself without distractions will give you a fresh start. Many adopt a morning routine and benefit greatly from it.

-        CHALLENGE YOURSELF THROUGHOUT THE DAY

Whether you are at university or in the office, you can set small targets like not checking your phone for the next 40 minutes. By doing this, you will become more productive while building your self-control. We aren't perfect, so it is only natural that we can't do this perfectly every time. When most people are bored, they immediately pull out their cell phones. Don't be like that! If you manage to use your devices consciously, you will not only have a lot more time freed up, but you will also experience better focus and higher motivation. Your inner child will slowly come out again!

COLD SHOWERS

Cold showers can be beneficial for many things. Some reports point towards that it can elevate mood, strengthen immune system function and increase alertness. [37] One thing is for sure; cold showers build self-discipline effectively. Starting, I recommend showering with warm water and then gradually turning the temperature down. Try to build your tolerance gradually and breathe heavily and controlled. Breathing the right way will make you tolerate cold water much better. Try to saturate your body with oxygen by breathing fully into your lungs. Look up Wim Hof Method to learn more about this practice.

MEDITATION

Meditation is a practice where a technique such as mindfulness is used to reach mental clearness and emotional stability. The only access you have to your life is the present moment. Unnecessary thoughts about the future and past are big sources of stress. You avoid having these big spikes of stress if you stay present. Meditation will help you with this. One of the biggest benefits of meditation is that it builds self-control. Self-control is crucial if you want to avoid porn or do nofap.

Meditation can improve attention and self-control as quickly as after just three hours of practice. Even though you may be unable to meditate effectively the first few times you try it, it is still a very effective practice. Meditation is furthermore shown to increase attention span, reduce stress and enhance self-awareness. Download an app for guided meditation and try it. By improving self-control and attention, you can perform better in many areas such as academia, work, recovery from addiction and so on. By doing meditation for 10-15 minutes every day, many benefits will arise that will help you in other areas of your life. Meditation can even replenish willpower to a certain extent, by quieting stressful thought loops. If your willpower is temporarily taxed, you can somewhat replenish it by meditating!

Meditation is furthermore shown to increase attention span, reduce stress and enhance self-awareness.

Meditation can even replenish willpower to a certain extent, by quieting stressful thought loops.

EXERCISE

Exercise is a fantastic thing for many reasons. Your health will improve drastically if you exercise consistently, and it is basically the closest thing to a wonder drug available for your willpower. Try to find something you enjoy, since consistency is key.

SOCIAL CHALLENGES

Challenging yourself socially is very important if you are not very outgoing by default. These challenges don't have to be dramatic. For instance, when you feel like speaking up and there is a little pressure, do it! It is your body trying to tell you the right action. Your DNA knows how to win. If you start to listen more to your instincts, you will become a more attractive person. Most likely, you experience at least one situation every day when you feel like speaking up or saying hi to someone and your heart skips a beat. Try to listen to your gut in these situations and go for it! Doing this will in the long run give you better relationships.

FIND ACCOUNTABILITY

The basic human need for approval and being consistent, can be used when trying to change a habit. If you tell your friends that you are trying to eat healthily, you add social pressure to yourself. Now, if you fail to live in alignment with your values, you have the judgment of other people to worry about as well. This can serve as an effective extra motivation. If we fail at a challenge like this, imagined scorn can be difficult to handle. So, a word of advice is to be a little careful before announcing something. Do it if you believe you can achieve it and you only need some extra motivation to pull through. The drive to stay consistent with what you publicize is a powerful effect. Use it to your advantage.

TRYING TO SUPPRESS UNWANTED THOUGHTS IS A REALLY BAD IDEA

One of the worst things you can do if you are recovering from addiction or trying to change unwanted behavior, is to go around all day thinking that you are never going to do that one thing ever again. It only makes unwanted thoughts persist. The best thing to do is to let go of the illusion of control. Permission to have unwanted thoughts makes unwanted thoughts less persistent.

Give up trying to stop thinking about porn. It is generally better to think about what we want, instead of what we don't want. If your only focus is trying to avoid porn, you are doing the same thing that dieters trying to restrict calories or certain foods are doing. On the other hand, if you focus on what you want to achieve (and you know that porn will affect that outcome negatively), you are much more likely to succeed. Focus on your goals instead of expending effort on trying to avoid porn consciously. By doing this, you will automatically be pulled away from it.

SELF-IMPROVEMENT

Make a commitment to yourself to become a better and more useful person every day. After a while, you can accomplish things that you never thought were possible. Constant improvement is necessary because remaining stagnant while time is passing by means declining. Your biological clock is ticking, and death is only coming closer. It is impossible to remain stagnant; you are either moving up or down. A 20-year-old person that has achieved nothing could be looked at as a person of potential. A 40-year-old person that has done nothing is a failure.

To avoid relapsing, you must change your day-to-day habits. If your current habits and behavior worked optimally, you wouldn't be reading this right now. There is no "secret" to avoiding porn. It is simply upgrading your day-to-day habits until they are so satisfying that you experience so much pleasure and fulfillment from them, that you don't have to rely on pleasure from porn or other shiny things. This process is not easy. It will be difficult at times, but if you stick to constant improvement with your big goal in mind, you can pull through. It is a marathon, not a race.

MORAL INCONGRUENCE

Moral incongruence is a major issue for many people. Many are unable to control their porn habits, and moral incongruence can be a driving force behind this. People that have grown up in religious or sexually conservative households can have strong negative feelings about porn. Some of these people feel guilty and ashamed of their behavior, but many continue to watch it, nonetheless. Higher levels of stress, anxiety, depression and diminished sexual well-being can occur when someone watches porn, despite believing that it is wrong or suboptimal behavior.

It is very important that your actions reflect your values. This is called behaving congruently. I would downplay the consequences of watching porn after a relapse. This is something that our brains do subconsciously in order to reduce the stress that is inflicted when we don't live up our goals and values. Being aware of this psychological mechanism is going to be helpful when trying to make a better life for yourself.

One of the reasons why we enjoy spending time with our closest friends so much, is that we behave congruently around them. We can be honest, open and speak our minds without worry. This is the best state to be in. To live a happy life, it is vital to strive towards congruent action in as many situations as possible. If you relapse, forgive yourself. No benefits come from beating yourself up too much. But if you fail, try to make sure it doesn't happen again by assessing what went wrong and resolve the issue.

It is very important that your actions reflect your values. This is called behaving congruently.

FOCUS ON THE MOST IMPORTANT THINGS

Willpower is like a muscle. If you exert your willpower on trying to avoid porn, you will likely find substitutes short-term. Some people replace bad habits with other ones. Trying to change many habits at once is taxing, and very few can do it successfully. Therefore, it is a good idea to take up a new habit and stick to it for a couple of weeks before adding more. You only have a certain amount of energy and focus, and if you expend this energy on 20 different habits every day, it can be difficult to chip away at the things that really matter. Use most of your focus and attention on the most important things to you.

BENEFITS FROM THAT OCCUR FROM AVOIDING PORN AND CONSCIOUS USE OF THE INTERNET:

- Better relationships

- Less anxiety

- Sharper mind

- Increased confidence

- More pleasure from everyday life

- More willpower

A naturally stabilized reward system is a reward well worth waiting for. The effects listed are what happens when you get there. Do you want 2 months with some pain or a lifetime of misery and decay? Every time you are failing to do what you know you are supposed to do, you are acquiring debt in the background of the opportunity cost of what you could have been. Face the discomfort right now and have a lifetime of results instead. Don't care about your short-time emotions. It is your long-term results that matter. Take action on the steps in this chapter right now. Reach your goals, not someone else's! If you are not working on your goals, you are a character in someone else's play.

KEY LESSONS

- People report on average that their relationships are the most important things in their life. Many people struggle with porn use or other addictions because they lack meaningful relationships. Pursue social challenges and try to build better relationships.

- Take conscious control of your digital use. If you manage to use the Internet consciously for the rest of your life, you will not relapse to Internet porn again, by default!

- Have a plan for every single day. Use your time productively.

- Willpower is something you can only work on at a time when it is not convenient for you.

- Reading will make you a more useful person. It will also build your focus and attention span. These attributes are beneficial when trying to quit porn and live a better life.

- Cold showers can elevate your mood, strengthen your immune system and increase your alertness.

- Meditation improves attention and self-control quickly.

- Challenge yourself every day by restricting cell phone or Internet use.

- Go outside your comfort zone.

CHAPTER 10: RELAPSES AND ENERGY SCALE

LOW POINTS

Low points are when you obtain the required motivation to change. It is not by every day of your life being perfect that you muster the necessary motivation to change. It is some degree of cognitive dissonance that enables us to step up. It doesn't have to be a bad situation necessarily, only worse than what is possible. Good habits repeated daily for an extended period equals success. Bad habits repeated daily for a long period equals failure.

At age 21, I lived at home with my parents and had nothing to show for. I was unemployed, didn't go to school and wasted my youthful moments. My outlook was bleak, and I didn't have any motivation whatsoever. My precious time was squandered. My only good habits were going to the gym 4 times a week and generally eating healthy. This was the time when I decide to do something about my situation. I ordered plane tickets to a different country and decided to backpack through Asia and Europe by myself. That was the turning point.

MICRO-DECISIONS

You get to vote 1000s of times every day how your life will be in the future. All these small micro-decisions may not seem important at the moment. It is precisely these decisions however, that determine your outcomes. The only difference between being wealthy, poor, fit and obese are the small choices you make 1000s of times every day. Most of us fail at the majority of these micro-decisions. These decisions can be things like, should I do the productive thing right now or wait one minute? Why not wait 2 more minutes? Pretty soon, time goes by and you are like damn, I should have spent my time doing something else instead. That time is forever gone now. These small moments are everything your life will ever be, and this is where success is achieved or not. This does not sound sexy, but it is a fact. The more of these micro-decisions you manage to delay gratification, the better your outcomes will be. If you double the number of good micro-decisions you do, you will get more things done. You more than double your results and have extra time to allocate towards something else.

You are fully responsible for your outcomes. This is a good thing because it means you can create the life you want if you are willing to put in the work. It is the accumulated effect of these small decisions that separate success from failure. Sometimes, you just have to do things you don't feel like doing.

You are fully responsible for your outcomes.

When you are first starting on your journey, most of these decisions are going to be suboptimal. A little progress can mean a world of difference. My first step was to start watching self-help content on YouTube. The content inspired me. As a result, I decided to step up and make a change. This is how you should spend the rest of your life: Trying to do better micro-decisions every day. And if there is reincarnation, do it again until you are dead.

This is how you should spend the rest of your life: Trying to do better micro-decisions every day. And if there is reincarnation, do it again until you are dead.

While I am writing this, I am currently an electrical engineer student. I have great academic results. I have traveled to different continents, seen different cultures and met many great people along the way. I have worked 3 years in sales and became good at it, despite my previous struggles with social anxiety. I have read dozens of books.

Changing a few small micro-decisions can change everything if you maintain the momentum. It is still going to be a gradual process, but small changes stack up over time. "Compound interest is the eighth wonder of the world" - Einstein. You get to vote 1000s of times every day what your life will be like in the future. Vote with your future in mind, not with what is convenient right now.

You get to vote 1000s of times every day what

your life will be like in the future. Vote with your future
in mind, not with what is convenient right now.

WHAT ARE USUALLY THE REASONS FOR RELAPSES?

I used to relapse because of a "perceived setback". This was a coping mechanism when things got difficult. I would feel like there was no point in avoiding porn at times since I wasn't making any progress. My main goal for a couple of years was to improve my social skills and become a better communicator. If I encountered a social situation where I felt "incompetent", I would often relapse afterward. Feeling helpless and apathetic is commonly a precursor to relapses. The key to avoiding relapses is to avoid going into these negative states of mind. Practicing gratitude can be very helpful to do this. Write down 5 things you are grateful for every single day. Personal examples include:

I am grateful that my health is good

I am grateful that I have a roof over my head

I am grateful I have enough money to eat

I am grateful for my friends and family

Writing these things down will keep your perspective healthy and ensure positivity. Memes and social media are made to make you experience cognitive dissonance. Suicide rates are at their lowest when there is a national crisis or war. If there is no problem, the human mind tends to invent one. Therefore, having a strong purpose is crucial. Your purpose will lead you down a path where difficulty and problems will arise. But since you chose that path, and hence also your problems, you will tackle them with enthusiasm.

Make a journal of progress. Whether you try to quit porn to

improve your social skills or excel academically, track your progress. Revisit your journal regularly and track the progress. This will reduce mental stress if you experience that from time to time. Gradual progression is very difficult to notice. Personally, my social skills increased dramatically by avoiding porn. Since the change happened gradually, I often didn't notice the change before relapsing.

The human brain is not good at picking up gradual change and subtle nuances. After relapsing, it became very clear that I had made immense progress, but it was completely wiped out after watching porn for hours. I would go back to being terribly stifled and unable to enjoy social encounters. So, a good way to make sure that you notice the progress you make is to track it! And if you see no tangible progress from journaling, it is time to make changes. The easiest way to notice this is if you write things down as well.

Another common reason for relapses is trying to fill a void. If you are unable to experience enough satisfaction from your everyday life when you quit porn, it is very easy to fall into this trap. What you want to do instead is to fill the void with new habits like reading, meditating, being social, traveling etc. At first, you may not have enough energy or courage to try these things out. Begin small and add new challenges with time if you resonate with this. Before you know it, you will find yourself in a better situation.

COMMON TRIGGERS BEFORE RELAPSING:

-       STRESS

Resolve this by finding a hobby to engage in when you are stressed out. Alternatively, you can try breathing exercises or meditation.

- NEGATIVE EMOTIONS

Mental health professionals can help you develop coping strategies. Emotions can generally be viewed as feedback on whether you are making progress towards your goals or not. If you chip away at your goals, you will experience fewer negative emotions. Emotions basically track whether you do what you are supposed to do or not, and how well you do it. Start taking massive action towards your goals and you will generally find yourself in a much better mood.

- EXPOSURE TO EXPLICIT CONTENT

Use a relaxation technique such as deep breathing for a couple of minutes. This enables you to regain control of your body.

ENERGY LEVELS

People experience different emotions and states of mind. These states fluctuate with emotion and life circumstances. For example, most people have experienced sadness due to the loss of a loved one. At a different time, they might have been happy and content. Depending on your "energy level" you perceive things differently. We all have some moods or states we find ourselves in the most. Depending on whether this is a positive or negative state, we have different amounts of energy available.

A more comprehensive model of the different states a person can experience is presented in Frederick Dodson's book Levels of Energy. He presents an energy scale ranging from 0-1000, where your state of consciousness increases as you move up. Moving up simply means to become happier. Emotions like guilt, apathy, fear, stress and anger are negative and reside lower than positive ones. Purpose, courage, love and happiness are among the positive ones.

Ascend from negative moods by embracing pain. The reason for this is that the natural state here is pain, and most people in low states constantly self-medicate to avoid inevitable pain. Think of people doing drugs, drinking excessively, gambling, watching too much porn and so on. These people generally do these things to alleviate pain in their lives. Unhappy people generally find a way to alleviate their suffering. The difference is how destructive their habits are. It's a world of difference between someone who plays World of Warcraft 5 hours a day and a heroin addict. What they have in common is that both are most likely running from and unable to face the discomfort.

Many people's habitual state is painful, and they avoid it by seeking out unnatural stimuli. Before change can happen though, the coping mechanism must be removed, and they have to face the discomfort. For a drug addict, this simply means to stop taking the drug. The next step is to allow the neurochemistry to adjust to a life without the addictive substance or behavior. Pain is inevitable at this stage since the brain has relied on the substance or behavior to feel good emotions. Suddenly it is taken away. The two components required to overcome this phase is faith (purpose) and willpower. Now you can perhaps see more clearly why the 3 questions exercise is so important.

The concept described in the previous paragraph applies to everyone (even people that are not addicts). If you want to become happier, you have to do the same thing. Restricting unnecessary stimuli will allow you to become more present and feel greater happiness from the small things in life. For a normal person, this can involve avoiding the temptation of ordering a burger at McDonald's. Resisting the temptation is not pleasurable short-term, but long-term their health will be much better. If you manage to become truly present and at ease at the moment, life will be beautiful anyway. The burger is simply not needed anymore. The point is this: Life can be so fulfilling by itself without all the distractions of Facebook, Instagram, junk food, porn, gambling etc. that you experience just as much or more pleasure by engaging in behavior that is not as stimulating. The only way to get there is to be conscious of what you allow in your life. Before you know it, simply walking down the street is enjoyable.

Life can be so fulfilling by itself without all the distractions of Facebook, Instagram, junk food, porn, gambling etc. that you experience just as much or even more pleasure by engaging in behavior that is not as stimulating.

How overstimulated we are, determine how much pleasure we get from the small things in life. When you feel stressed out after work and your brain really wants a dopamine hit, don't allow it. Sit down and meditate instead. Before you know it, you become relaxed and present. Suddenly, the dopamine hit seems unnecessary and you work without distractions towards your goals. If you are in a compulsive state of mind, restricting stimuli can be painful and almost impossible. Immense progress can be made rapidly when we try to become less reliant on stimuli every day.

People who are residing at a low level of consciousness, experience pain and negativity daily. When you live like this, porn use or things like playing video games compulsively, can temporarily make you feel better. The only way to quit compulsive behavior permanently is to ascend your consciousness to a higher level, where you derive more happiness from daily activities. To get there, you simply have to accept pain in the short-term by removing the crutch. In the long term, you will have a fantastic life.

ENERGY LADDER

Positive energy

Love

Purpose

Desire

Courage

Negative energy

Anger

Fear

Grief

Apathy

This energy ladder is only a model, and it is not a scientifically accurate representation. It is a good way to describe the difference between various states that people find themselves in. The higher up this ladder you go, the more energy and positivity you have. People in apathy for instance, will have more energy available if they move up to victimhood and blame, which is around fear energetically. "It is not your fault; it is the government's fault". For people in apathy, this is excellent advice. For people in fear, it is good advice to become angry, as they have more energy at their disposal here.

Something I experienced a lot myself was going from an angry state (which was my default at one point) into apathy after experiencing an awkward social encounter, which was most of them for honestly. What usually happens is that if we don't express our emotions, we descend. Porn use resides somewhere around fear, according to Dodson in Levels of Energy. What happens when you go down into apathy is that porn has higher energy than your state of consciousness, which will make it almost impossible to avoid. This is not scientifically proven at all, but a good mental model to adopt.

Try to catch yourself if you feel like you are heading down into lower moods. Simply being aware of this energy scale, will make you more capable of handling your emotions. So, if you manage to avoid permanently going into lower states of consciousness, your chance of relapsing will be dramatically lowered. For this reason, learning to control your emotions better can be extremely beneficial. This is the case whether you try to quit porn, any addiction or change any unwanted behavior. We access different belief structures based on our mood.

Everyone has different belief structures, and we want to permanently access the positive ones, where we have more energy at our disposal. If we constantly live in alignment with our values and goals, we will automatically be in a better mood and state of mind. A lot of distress and negative emotions come from doing things we know we shouldn't be doing. Do the stuff you are supposed to do, and it will be much easier to avoid porn or other harmful things.

REFLECTIONS ON STIMULI

You can actively increase your enjoyment from life, by reducing your exposure to overstimulating content. I think drugs make the point. Most people that eventually turn into drug addicts, start with alcohol, then marijuana. They try harder drugs and get less high from their drug of choice as time goes by. In the end, some end up addicted to heroin or meth. At this point, existence by itself is extremely painful and the only way to alleviate pain is by getting high. This basically means that exposure to a more extreme stimulus, makes us decline. On the other hand, meditation is a commonly used practice to become more spiritual and ascend "spiritually".

Needing less stimulation means that we become happier. Meditation is basically a practice where we try to find as much enjoyment as possible from simply being alive without any stimuli. I think this makes the point. Reducing the stimuli we allow in our lives, can make us happier. This is why we have to be so conscious of our use of the Internet, TV, porn, candy, gambling etc. Don't just meditate and overstimulate yourself for the rest of your day, be aware 24/7. The people that are the happiest find the small things in life valuable. This happens if your neurochemistry is healthy and balanced. Good amounts of neurotransmitters should be released from doing simple things. That is only going to happen if you make a conscious effort to avoid extreme and unnatural stimuli.

KEY LESSONS

-       You get to vote 1000s of times every day how your life is going to be in the future. Vote with your future in mind, not with what is convenient right now.

-       Relapses usually happen as coping mechanisms or to fill a void. Take on new challenges and hobbies. It is going to be difficult, but a month of pain is worth it to have a lifetime of results.

-       Practice gratitude daily, this will keep your mood elevated.

-       Addiction normally develops when people try to self-medicate pain. Pain must be accepted and embraced to overcome it.

CHAPTER 11: ACHIEVEMENT AND NEUROCHEMISTRY

You can experience more pleasure from artificial sources than from real life. If you only plan for 3 weeks, you should probably do heroin. If you plan to stick around longer, you should avoid it. The pleasure of artificial things like drugs and porn have a steep cost. Excelling in real life is going to give you pleasure, in addition to inner satisfaction.

The satisfaction that comes from doing hard things and sticking to your plan through adversity is well worth it. This is real confidence by the way. Confidence is not something you can attain by thinking or playing mind games with yourself. Confidence comes from doing hard things that most others would simply not do. Bill Gates has said that you don't deserve confidence by merely being born. You must do something before you deserve to feel good about yourself. Looking yourself in the mirror and being proud of yourself is indescribable.

Substitutes for real-life can be pleasurable for short periods. You will have to face some pain to build your life if you currently play video games for hours every day. Some people succumb to short-term pleasures because they cannot picture a better future for themselves. It is always at the darkest right before dawn. Remember this. The way I got out of the rut was by taking one step at a time. I fumbled for a long time. Over a few years, I managed to make progress, even though I had some difficult periods. Things may feel hopeless, but do not give up.

Low periods might even be good for you in the long run, crazy as it sounds. The greatest leaders of all time like Winston Churchill, Franklin Roosevelt and Abraham Lincoln did not grow to be that great by dancing on roses. They suffered immensely and managed to build resilience as a result. Both Abraham Lincoln and Winston Churchill were suicidal at some points in their lives. Abraham Lincoln had a serious depression in his early adulthood. Now he is remembered as the greatest president of all time, and one of the greatest men in history. If you manage to pull through these difficult times, you will get out on the other side a much stronger person. You will have a much greater understanding of human psychology and much greater empathy and awareness of how and why different people behave in certain ways than most. Winston Churchill, Franklin Roosevelt and Abraham Lincoln managed to lead effectively in times of crisis because they had experienced hardship. Don't think that you have "wasted a period of your life" if that time was spent in depression. You are most likely only going to be humbler and more grateful for what you have later on.

HAPPINESS

Happiness is something that must come from a foundation of strength. Not every moment of your life is going to be fantastic. It is great if your life is enjoyable and you have a deep and intimate relationship with your partner. What are you going to do when your partner is on a business trip and are forced to spend time alone? Cry like a baby because you are forced to be alone for a few days? Browse through social media in perpetuity? Are you going to watch porn obsessively for hours to replace the dopamine spikes you are craving?

To be happy in the moments that really matter, you have to endure some uncomfortable moments in between. When you accept this, everything will become much easier. If you manage to live this way for some time, you will find that your overall quality of life will increase drastically. Some part of your day is going to be painful no matter what. Accept this now. You can either accept it or try to run away from it, only making it worse in the future. If you do your commute in complete silence and force yourself to not rely on stimuli during parts of your day, you will find that the stimuli you experience later are much more enjoyable. Allow yourself some pleasure but remove as much unnecessary pleasure as possible. Before you know it, the small things in life will give you massive satisfaction and pleasure.

To be happy in the moments that really matter, you have to endure some uncomfortable moments in between.

From personal experience, I increase my sociability by avoiding TV and social media. The reason is most likely that too much exposure to these things fulfill some of our social needs. This is why we are drawn to TV, social media, Internet, etc. to such a large extent. They provide stimuli that we find valuable. The danger occurs when these stimuli make us less likely to seek out real friendship and social encounters. This trend has already our impacted lives massively.

NEUROCHEMISTRY FOR HAPPINESS

Happiness is for many rare due to the competing influences of depression and anxiety. Studies conclude that the genetic importance of happiness is ranging from 35 to 50 %. Neuroscience studies have shown that some parts of the brain control happiness (amygdala, limbic system and hipocamp.) These studies have also shown that neurotransmitters play a role in determining levels of happiness (dopamine, serotonin, norepinephrine and endorphins). Other studies have pointed towards that the adrenal gland – responsible for adrenaline and cortisol and the pituitary gland – responsible for the secretion of oxytocin, contributes to happiness. [38] Our level of happiness is a result of several different factors. Two of the most important neurotransmitters for happiness are dopamine and serotonin.

DOPAMINE

Dopamine plays a role in the brain's reward system, helping reinforce behavior that can result in a reward. Low levels of dopamine are linked to procrastination, self-doubt and low enthusiasm. Porn use causes huge spikes in dopamine. This results in lower dopamine responses from other activities.

SEROTONIN

Serotonin is to a big extent, responsible for your mood. It is possible to increase levels of serotonin through regularly challenging yourself. Winning creates a positive feedback loop that builds higher levels of serotonin. This results in higher self-esteem and less insecurity. Gratitude practices increase serotonin also. Our brain has trouble telling the difference between what is real and imagined. Therefore, writing things down that you appreciate and are grateful for can be very impactful. Reliving a pleasant experience can also be helpful.

Loneliness and depression can appear when serotonin is absent. On the other hand, it is abundant when you feel powerful and important. Challenging yourself and following through, will boost your serotonin. This will make it easier for you to avoid porn as you will become happier and less reliant on porn for good emotions.

CORTISOL

Cortisol is the body's main stress hormone and it is a consistent marker for depression. Individuals with higher levels of purpose in life register lower and more stable levels of cortisol and adrenaline. [38] It is not clear whether porn use affects cortisol. Many people report that they feel uncomfortable and stressed in social encounters after porn sessions, which can be explained by increased levels of cortisol. Connection with other people reduces cortisol and staying at home masturbating to a screen doesn't exactly make us more connected.

Individuals with higher levels of purpose in life register lower and more stable levels of cortisol and adrenaline.

OXYTOCIN

Oxytocin aids happiness by being beneficial for social relationships. It is directly linked to human bonding and increased trust and loyalty. With the direction the world is heading in with more screen time, it is more important than ever to have people to spend time with. Humans are social creatures. There is a reason we have cities with millions of people. Oxytocin makes us feel close and bonded with others when it is released. It is reported as being quite important for our happiness. There is a big difference however, between masturbating to porn and having sex because oxytocin is released with human contact.

CONCLUSION

Porn use affects many of the most important neurotransmitters for happiness negatively. There is also a big difference between the hormonal impact of masturbation and sex. After sex, much higher levels of prolactin are released than after masturbation (for men). Prolactin combats the depressing effect that overuse of the dopamine system has. Excessive masturbation can furthermore result in lower testosterone levels.

From personal experience, my mood has stabilized massively after ending porn use. This is something that many other people have reported as well: elevated and more stable moods after ending porn use (and nofap). I hope that more research will be done in the future on how porn use affects us. Right now, it is pretty clear that it affects us negatively, but to what extent is still unclear. There is a big experiment going on right now with porn's ease of access.

KEY LESSONS

-       Having gone through difficult experiences can be a good thing. The difficult periods in Churchill's life helped him be the great leader he was during WW2.

-       Failure is a good learning experience if you allow yourself to learn from it.

-       Some part of your day is going to be painful no matter what. To be happy in the moments that matter, you have to endure some uncomfortable situations in between. The sooner you accept this, the better. Often, trying to run away from pain is what leads to ruined lives.

-       Porn use affects many of our most important neurotransmitters for happiness negatively.

CHAPTER 12: HOW TO GO FORWARD

Success is a highly subjective thing for different people. For some, success means fancy cars, world travel, having an abundant dating life and huge piles of money. For others, success means being respected and being a person of integrity. And still, others value having a loving family they can bond and share good experiences with. What is the common denominator between all these people that are successful in their respective ways? Is there a common trait that all these people embody?

QUALITIES REQUIRED TO EXCEL IN LIFE:

- Ability to maintain focus for prolonged periods.

- Willpower. The ability to work hard towards your goals.

- Ambition and knowing what you want.

- Patience.

- Integrity.

- Connecting and ability to communicate well. Surround yourself with likeminded people that want to achieve similar things in their lives.

These qualities are commonly reported as being important to achieving success. Avoiding porn or doing nofap can help you attain these qualities.

You will generally receive in return what you put out into the world. If you do bad things and make the lives of other people worse, you will probably feel bad about yourself. On the other hand, if you try to make other people's lives better, you will be compensated handsomely. The most important thing happens on the inside. You will feel better about yourself if you make other people's lives better. And you should. You want to adopt this model if nothing else than for your selfish best interest.

Inner changes will happen if you do good things. For me, adopting this way of thinking and acting on it was helpful when trying to quit porn as well. If nothing else, it made me feel better about myself, which resulted in fewer "low points". Like we all know, feeling down makes it easy to turn to the comfort of porn.

The way you feel about yourself will be approximately equivalent to the positive or negative impact you have on the world. If you impact the lives of other people negatively, you are probably going to feel bad. If you make other people's lives better, you will probably feel pretty good about yourself.

SOCIAL SKILLS AND COMMUNICATION

Some skills that are useful to learn no matter what field you go into. The most important of these is social skills. People that are promoted the fastest aren't necessarily those who are just good at their jobs. The people that get ahead the fastest are those who are good workers and have good social skills. So, what does having good social skills mean? If you manage to make people around you feel good, they want to be around you more. That is just how the world works. If you possess great social skills and excel in your chosen specialty, you will rise quickly and become successful.

No matter your profession, intelligence or level of success in life, you will pay a big price if you don't build good social skills. Ignaz Semmelweis figured out that it was possible to cut the incidence of childbed fever dramatically by the use of hand disinfection. This happened in the 19th Century. In other words, Semmelweis was a man that changed the world for the better by contributing to a major medical breakthrough. You would think he would be appreciated and honored in his life. The sad part of the story is that Semmelweis died a lonely and depressed man, very early.

People generally resist change because of comfort. Semmelweis lacked the social intelligence to understand that confronting commonly held beliefs head-on would result in confrontation. He told other doctors that they were killing people by not using hand disinfectants. He was right, but because of his lacking social understanding, he made many enemies along the way. Eventually, more people died than necessary before his views were adopted. If he had been less confrontational and delivered his views in a more socially calibrated way, not only would his own life have turned out better, but fewer people would have died from contracting unnecessary infections at hospitals. Semmelweis' lack of social skills ruined his life.

Mastering our chosen specialties is great, but social skills are the medium we use to convey our beliefs and brilliance. If your social skills are currently not up to par, don't worry, it is possible to fix it.

Non-verbal cues make up 93 % of communication. [39] Body-language is the most important factor followed by tonality. One good way to increase your outcomes in life is by being sure of your leadership. Avoiding porn is going to help you in this area. A common side effect of nofap and avoiding porn is feeling more at ease in social encounters. This will make your non-verbal communication better, which will hugely impact your overall communication. Since communication is how we relate to other people, and the universally ranked most important aspect of people's life is their relationships, avoiding porn can make your life tangibly better.

Political correctness is the death of sexiness. There is a very important dynamic to be aware of in terms of communication. This is the different communication styles that should be used in professional environments and elsewhere. Authenticity is required in order to make real connections with other people. In professional work environments, authenticity is not always the best style of communication. Think of it like you are being compensated for behaving a certain way to fit into the corporation. Don't let this affect your personality away from work.

Being politically correct means that the content you deliver is meant to offend no one. Therefore, it will be completely absent of actual content. When you engage with the real world, you should strive to communicate in an authentic and real way. This means that some people will be offended by what you say from time to time. This is completely natural, and it is to be expected since we are different! There are 7,8 billion people on earth (2020). If you say something that offends no one, there is no actual content in your message. The way to convey your personality is to be completely honest but calibrated. Strive to reach the state Gandhi described as happiness: "Happiness is when what you think, say and do are in harmony".

> *"Happiness is when what you think, say and do are in harmony"* – Gandhi.

ABILITY TO TOLERATE SOCIAL PRESSURE

Tolerating social pressure is also extremely important. This is required to become a successful investor, entrepreneur, a great communicator and a lot of other things. In order to become a successful investor, it is important to stay cool and trust your judgment, and not let the psychology of the masses influence you. This is the case if you want to live in alignment with your values as well. People that want to stop watching porn, will commonly have to face social discomfort when expanding their comfort zone. Accept this sooner rather than later.

Whenever an opportunity to practice negotiation arises, take it. If the waiter brings you the wrong meal, let them know. Dare to speak up! Failure to do so will ensure that your life will be a mess. If you can't negotiate something small or face a little social pressure, how are you going to be able to live in alignment with your values when your peer group tries to pressure you into doing something you don't want? Don't be a dick but have firm boundaries and let people know when they cross them.

WORK

A person that values his or her short-term emotions above their long-term goals will pay for it. They are going to be a slave essentially for the rest of their lives. Focus on 1 or 2 main projects and spend most of your time on these things. People that try to do everything well, will do exactly zero things well. What is Michael Phelps good at? Swimming. What is Warren Buffet good at? Investing. Try to find the synergies between the things you use your time on and draw it all together. My main goal right now is to achieve financial freedom to be able to help people more effectively later in life. To get there, I do different things like reading books, studying, working on my social skills etc. When you find your big goal for the future and re-engineer it into smaller steps, magic will happen. Suddenly, it doesn't feel like work anymore to chip away at your goals and stay on the grind.

"To get what you want, you have to deserve what you want. The world is not yet a crazy enough place to reward a bunch of undeserving people" – Charles T. Munger.

KEY LESSONS

-        Avoiding porn will help you embody the personality traits required to excel in life.

-        Make yourself useful to other people. This is the easiest way to get what you want. I don't believe in karma, but there is a correlation between what you put out into the world and what you receive.

-        Prioritize learning social skills. Regardless of what you want to do with your life, being able to communicate well will be extremely important.

-        Tolerating social pressure is important. Find your values and live in alignment with them.

-        To have excellent outcomes, you must engage in excellent behavior. You generally get what you deserve.

FINAL THOUGHTS

Hopefully, you go back to your life after reading this with a higher awareness of how mindless digital activity impacts lives. Too much digital use impacts our neurochemistry and takes away our most precious asset; our time. Many people growing up these days don't go through the maturation process properly before they take control of their digital lives. It can seem overwhelming and almost frightening to have all the opportunities we have access to in the 21st century. I hope you have achieved some clarity on how you should spend your time going forward as well.

"Don't be afraid your life will end; be afraid it will never begin" - Grace Hansen.

Good luck. Stay strong!

If you found this book helpful, please consider leaving an honest review. It is only by spreading the word that we can help more people realize the negative impact porn use and overstimulation can have on lives.

- Havard Mela

CITATIONS

WHY IS PORN HARMFUL?

[1] https://www.theguardian.com/comment-isfree/2018/dec/30/internet-porn-says-more-about-ourselves-than-technology

[2] https://www.nationalobserver.com/2019/07/11/news/net-flix-and-online-porn-cause-much-pollution-entire-countries-report-says

[3] https://www.inquisitr.com/3441111/porn-watching-by-married-couples-jacks-divorce-risk-rate-up-nearly-200-percent/

[4] https://www.therecoveryvillage.com/process-addiction/porn-addiction/related/pornography-statistics/#gref

[5] https://www.lukesniewski.com/wp-content/uploads/2018/08/The-assessment-and-treatment-of-adult-hetero-sexual-men-with-self-perceived-problematic-pornography-use-A-review.pdf

[6] Yuri Tomikawa, "No Sex, Please, We're Young Japanese Men," The Wall Street Journal, January 13, 2011.

[7] O'Sullivan, Lucia, L. Brotto, E. Byers, J. Majerovich, J. Wuest. "Prevalence and Characteristics of Sexual Functioning Among Sexually Experienced Middle to Late Adolescents." The Journal of Sexual Medicine 11, no. 3 (2014): 630–41.

[8] Foresta, Carlo. "Sessualita Mediatica e Nuove Forme Di Patologia Sessuale Campione 125 Giovani Maschi." ("Sexuality Media and New Forms of Sexual Pathology Sample 125 Young Males, 19–25 Years")

[9] https://www.ncbi.nlm.nih.gov/pmc/articles/PMC5040517/

[10] Simone Kühn and Jürgen Gallinat, "Brain Structure and Func-

tional Connectivity Associated with Pornography Consumption: The Brain on Porn." JAMA Psychiatry (2014): 827–34.

[11] Ine Beyers, Laura Vandebosch, and Steven Eggermont, "Early Adolescent Boys' Exposure to Internet Pornography: Relationships to Pubertal Timing, Sensation Seeking, and Academic Performance," Journal of Early Adolescence (2015).

[12] https://www.theatlantic.com/health/archive/2014/01/how-sex-affects-intelligence-and-vice-versa/282889/

[13] Jennifer P. Schneider, "Effects of Cybersex Addiction on the Family: Results of a Survey," Sexual Addiction & Compulsivity 7, nos. 1 and 2 (2000): 31–58.

[14] Pamela Paul, "From Pornography to Porno to Porn: How Porn Became the Norm," in The Social Costs of Pornography, edited by James R. Stoner Jr. and Donna M. Hughes, 3–20. Princeton, New Jersey: Witherspoon Institute, 2010.

[15] Vincent Cyrus Yoder, Thomas B. Virden III, and Kiran Amin, "Internet Pornography and Loneliness: An Association?" Sexual Addiction & Compulsivity 12, no. 1 (2005): 19–44.

[16] Richard Barry, former president of the American Academy of Matrimonial Lawyers, as quoted in Pamela Paul, "From Pornography to Porno to Porn: How Porn Became the Norm," in The Social Costs of Pornography, edited by James R. Stoner Jr. and Donna M. Hughes, 3–20. Princeton, New Jersey: Witherspoon Institute, 2010.

WILLPOWER

[17] https://www.ncbi.nlm.nih.gov/pmc/articles/PMC5626575/

[18] https://www.ncbi.nlm.nih.gov/pmc/articles/PMC4073202/

[19] https://www.ncbi.nlm.nih.gov/pmc/articles/PMC3680351/

[20] https://www.ncbi.nlm.nih.gov/pmc/articles/PMC6701263/

[21] https://www.ncbi.nlm.nih.gov/pmc/articles/PMC1805733/

COGNITIVE BIASES

[22] https://www.ncbi.nlm.nih.gov/pmc/articles/PMC6129743/

[23] https://www.ncbi.nlm.nih.gov/pmc/articles/PMC6224065/

[24] https://www.ncbi.nlm.nih.gov/pmc/articles/PMC5606704/

[25] https://en.wikipedia.org/wiki/Hyperbolic_discounting

[26] https://www.nejm.org/doi/full/10.1056/NEJMsa066082

[27] https://www.ncbi.nlm.nih.gov/pmc/articles/PMC3858579/

[28] https://www.ncbi.nlm.nih.gov/pmc/articles/PMC3213002/

SUPERNORMAL STIMULUS

[29] https://www.ncbi.nlm.nih.gov/pmc/articles/PMC4600144/

ADDICTION

[30] https://www.ncbi.nlm.nih.gov/pmc/articles/PMC4677151/

[31] https://www.ncbi.nlm.nih.gov/pmc/articles/PMC6352245/

[32] https://www.ncbi.nlm.nih.gov/pmc/articles/PMC5039517/

WHO ARE YOU?

[33]   https://www.nytimes.com/2007/07/25/health/25iht-fat.4.6830240.html

HOW TO TAKE CONSCIOUS CONTROL OF YOUR HABITS

[34] https://www.medicalnewstoday.com/articles/320265

[35] https://www.ncbi.nlm.nih.gov/pubmed/12659241

[36] https://www.ncbi.nlm.nih.gov/pubmed/8560313

[37] https://www.medicalnewstoday.com/articles/325725#increased-alertness

ACHIEVEMENT AND NEUROCHEMISTRY

[38] https://www.ncbi.nlm.nih.gov/pmc/articles/PMC4449495/

[39]   https://www.nytimes.com/2006/09/24/books/chapters/0924-1st-peas.html